ABOUT THE AUTHOR

Basil Onyejuruwa is fondly referred to as Basil Onye is a priest of the Catholic Diocese of Okigwe Nigeria. He is from Nunya, Isuikwuator in Abia State Nigeria.

Education:

Elementary School: Ansarudeen Primary School Lagos and St. Paul's Primary School Nunya, Abia State Nigeria

Secondary School: City Basic School Lagos/Marshal Business School Okigwe/Immaculate Conception Minor Seminary, Umuahia, Abia State, Nigeria

Tertiary Education:

Nativity Spiritual Year Seminary Umuahia/ The Seat of Wisdom Major Seminary Owerri – Pontifical Urban University Rome: Philosophical Studies

The University of Santo Tomas Espana Philippines: AB Degree in Theological Studies and Licentiate Degree or Master Degree in Canon Law

Teacher Certificate of Education St. Paul University Quezon City Philippines

Master of Arts in Education Management and Doctor of Education Leadership from the National Teachers' College, Manila

Ph.D. Industrial Psychology Eulogio Amang Rodriguez Institute of Science and Technology

Hobby: Playing Soccer/ Playing Lawn tennis/ Playing Music/Preaching/ Giving Retreats and Counseling/ Listen to News and World Affairs.

Principle/ Philosophy of Life: Good knowledge brings about worthy confidence for a noble living.

Prayer principle: Give me strength Lord, against your enemies!

ACKNOWLEDGEMENT

I will like to acknowledge all my friends, especially those who encouraged this work in every way and those I have had a brain-storming session with, who encouraged me to put my ideas into writing.

DEDICATION

I dedicate this book to everyone who loves my country Nigeria and to everyone who spends tangible time and resources, thinking, learning and doing stuff in order to ramp the greatness of this country.

TABLE OF CONTENTS

Page

ACKNOWLEDGEMENT	i

DEDICATION ii

ABSTRACT iii

CHAPTER 1

Introduction 1

Commentary on the Chronology of Nigerian History
The Scramble for West Africa 14
British Federalized Nigeria 19
The Nigerian Self-Rule 21
The Nigerian Leadership Approach 24

CHAPTER 2
The Haphazard Federalist Style of Nigerian
Government 38
The Indirect Rule System 39
Autonomy as Yakubu Gowon's Reason
for the 12 States Division 40
Gowon and Ojukwu and the Aburi Meeting 45
The Declaration of Secession and the Civil War 54

CHAPTER 3
The Slapdash of Capitalist and Socialist Economic
Style 89
The Social Market Economy 105
The Nigerian Economic Plan 108
Social Economics, Social Capital, Social Market
in Nigeria 112
Systemic Exploitation 118

CHAPTER 4
The Human Capital Resources/Education 128
Integral Education in Nigeria 141
Values, Life Style and Social Affairs – Education

Matters	166
The Nigerian Socio-Economic Affairs	176
Education and Social Strategies	181

CHAPTER 5
Proposed Leverage: Security Socio-Political and Economic

Federalize and Modernize	188
Characteristics of Democratic	192
Commitment-Process for Democratization and Modernization	195
Decentralize the Command Source of Nigerian Police	207
Decongest the Center	214
Appendix	218
References	237

ABSTRACT

TITLE : ONE FEDERALIZED NATION

Strong with Variety and Diversity,
Rich in Human Capital-Resources and (One)
Indivisible

The title of this book appears in Part 1 of Chapter 1 of the Constitution of the Federal Republic of Nigeria 1999. The introductory part of the Constitution contains the words "One and Indivisible" and indissoluble sovereign nation under God.

Nigeria, is a country in West Africa, it has a border with Niger in the north. It has Chad in the northeast. It has Cameroon in the east and Benin in the west. Its coast in the south is located on the Gulf of Guinea in the Atlantic Ocean.

Nigeria was a British colony. Nigeria attained her independence and federation on October 1 1960 under a constitution that provided for a parliamentary government and a substantial measure of self-government for the country's three regions.

The British indirect rule system was the indirect leadership which prepared the Nigerian leadership system towards greater autonomy to the three regions which afterwards was split into twelve states. General Gowon rightly mentioned as his aim in mind for dividing Nigeria three regions into twelve states was the attainment of greater autonomy for the twelve states. Gowon had an oversight in his leadership; he repealed the basic aim which recognized the variety and diversity in the greater autonomy of the twelve states by establishing a unitary system of government and paying only lip service to the substantial autonomy or self-government of the twelve states which was original with the British.

The basic principle which established federalism as a model for modern government recognized a country which has variety, diversity and multi-culture and language and ethnic cleavage and Nigeria is one of such. The British system of governance is unique with the United Kingdom and the British advocate for the federal system of governance for Nigeria which must give autonomy and self-government to the regional states in recognition of Nigerian ethnic diversity.

> That country, which is, I remind the House again, the most populous State in the continent of Africa, is, of course, extraordinarily diverse in race, religion and in social and economic development. Therefore, it is not in the least surprising that the political development it has chosen is that of a Federation in three regions, with each region self-governing in its own concerns.

The value attached to the federalist model is implied in the unchallenged development and advancement of such countries like the United States of America, Canada, and European Union, Australia and Russia to mention but a few. Because of the hypocritical leadership attitude towards federalism and autonomy to the states in Nigeria; the Nigerian central and unitary form of governance has stifled innovation, creative ability, leadership skill, sense of belonging and above all has failed to benefit from the full measure of ethnic diversity and variety of the regions and individuals. It has made the center of governance the center of everything such that the state governors move to-and-from Abuja for the states' allocation. Many corrupt practices are consequent upon the fact of central authority governance; everything is coming and moving to the center. Lagos State was the former capital territory and center of everything and because of the congestion of Lagos the new capital territory was shifted to Abuja and soon Abuja will be over congested. Federalism as a system of government permits that substantial autonomy should be given to regional states so that they can develop at their pace.

Since 1966 Nigeria has been ruled by the military except for a few years when the country noticed civilian democratic rule until 1999. All the military takeovers cited that the reason for their takeover was that the previous regime or republic was corrupt, aimless, and autocratic and lacked leadership. Of course a country with such magnitude of population, variety and diversity cannot successfully be governed by the center without creating a magnitude of illusion and leadership failure.

From the chronology of Nigerian history and leadership there is a self-revealing leadership failure on a high scale; a blistering failure to build the legacy of the country on the posterity; failure to recognize the talents and aspiration of the citizens; a learning failure that made trivial of the ethnic diversity and the civil war. There has been consistent and willful praise of divisive politics and sowing the seed of hostility and violence that Nigerians have long lost the sense of value, social cohesion and cohabitation, loss of confidence and trust with one another and with little or no optimism or enthusiasm for what the future may hold. The Nigerian education system has long suffered the negligence of the leaders to fund education. The process has also failed to recognize the human capital resources as priceless investment. It places value on education in terms of money rather than political advancement and contribution towards social cohesion. There are little or no traces of the historical past in the curriculum of schools. There is a continuing disproportionate gap between the rich and the poor in Nigerian economy; and Nigerians have compromised moral quintessence for an easy lifestyle. Many Nigerians chose to seek greener pastures through migration because they feel they are not safe in Nigeria and their aspirations are not protected. Many Nigerians have faced untold hardship and many died because of the hardship they faced in their desire to get beyond the shores of Nigeria.

Among the problems facing Nigeria is the dearth of resources among the thirty six states and how to distribute fairly what is available. Another challenge is the poor security system, unstable economy, self interest partisan politicians and lack of leadership; these factors were doubly recurring dating back from the Nigerian independence till present and become perennial agitation.

The entire Nigerian environment is a flicker of agitation. Agitation is part of peoples' demonstration of democratic and human rights and yearning of the people against poverty, marginalization and absence of opportunity, presence of violence, historic learning failure and leadership failure. This book reflects on all the leadership crises and the agitation of Nigerians since 1930s; the Jos riot of 1932 and 1945, the Kano riot of 1953 and 1956, the massacre of the Igbo people in 1966, the 1966 riots started by the Institute of Management and the students of Ahmadu Bello University Jos, the Aburi meeting of January 4 and 5 1967, the faction against Aburi, the mistake of Emeka Odimegwu Ojukwu in the declaration of secession and the Civil War and the mistake of Yakubu Gowon's leadership.

On July 25-28, 1961 he Nigerian first Prime Minister visited the United States of America. He had one of the greatest reception American government has given to any foreign black leader. Sir Abubakar Tafawa Balewa was called to address the US House of Representatives. He spoke few words on freedom, liberty and democracy and promised the world that never will the light of creative and initiative freedom, altruistic liberty and patriotic democracy dim or weaken in Nigeria.

People cannot walk away from their history but they can "rewrite" it by adapting in positive ways. Individuals are inseparable from their history and they can shape it.

This book proposed some leverage; that the history of Nigeria may be taught at the primary and secondary levels of education. The Nigerian education may consider among its priorities the pursuit of integral education.

The Nigerian Socio-economic Reality

The Nigerian social market economy may refrain from willful exploitation, plan, and guide and fix production, the workforce, or sales; far from any advocacy for chaos; it should support planned efforts to positively influence the economy through the organic means of a comprehensive economic policy forged with flexible adaptation to market behavior and studies. By combining monetary, credit, trade, tax, customs, investment and social policies as well as other measures, this type of economic policy must aim to create an economy for Nigerians to serve the welfare and needs of the entire population and by so doing fulfill the ultimate goal of providing opportunity for young and growing investors and quell the syndrome of get-rich-overnight. Since the economy of Nigeria has two Phases: the capitalist and the communist. There are some areas of the pattern where it is allowed for free market and competition and there are some areas that are not free for all, the government itself owns or controls those areas. This is an interaction between capitalism and communalism and such an economic system is plausible to ensure growth, hard work, and stability and to control undue forces and frustration of free market initiative; it is a kind of mixed economy. However, it is still difficult to evaluate the success of such an economic style based on which of these systems has protected the wealth of the country more from selfish-interest or how both have helped in yielding economic advancement in the country. The leadership and the government may have to review the corporate and business environment of Nigeria.

The slapdash economic plans results because of the centripetal economic policies that aims at "fixing"; there is synthetic attempts to determine market forces and behavior of the people; there is exploitation; until the two hinges of capitalist and communalist economy are reframed to fit the principles dictating for federalist states the economy would remain stagnated.

There is Need for Milestone Police Reform

There is a need for governance reforms from the center to the states level. There is a need for police reforms. How may the

Nigerian Police force be reformed to gain the public trust, depoliticized and be rid of corruption? The best leverage would be to decentralize the command source of the Nigerian Police Force so that the State sectors and the Local Community units may be part of the security system by working side by side with the Police.

For too long the Nigerian economy has fallen prey to many intransigent and lack of transparent presidents who made advantage of the unitary and central system of authority and governance and defrauded the entire country of its natural and human resources.

This book therefore advocates and proposed for full "Federation" for Nigerian government following the 1999 Constitution:

> Chapter I General Provisions Part I Federal Republic of Nigeria 2. (1) Nigeria is one indivisible and indissoluble sovereign state to be known by the name of the Federal

Republic of Nigeria. (2) Nigeria shall be a Federation consisting of States and a Federal Capital Territory.

Nigerian leadership may consider complete federation as the best leverage that would transform the country into a fast developing and stable economy, reform the Police Force through decentralizing of the command source, give state governments full right to develop and contribute their proportional share to the federal government. States that lack resources may receive loans from the federal government or extend their hands with solidarity to be helped by neighboring states. Complete federation would make wealth of the variety and diversity of the ethnic cleavage and such would make for a win-win condition of leadership trustworthiness, mutual satisfaction, sense of belonging and bring back the Nigerian pride of being African most talented nation, most viable economy, strongest military, and the country with the most integrated education and this is the time for harnessing the Nigerian variety, multi-religious advantage, ethnic diverse reality and one indivisible Nigeria.

INTRODUCTION

How has the Nigerian social and economic affairs affected the entire Nigerian environment and the lifestyle of the people? This question would lead to a critical reflection of the chronology of Nigerian history, Nigerian leadership approach, and the haphazard federalist style of Nigerian government; the slapdash of capitalist and socialist economic style and the perennial agitation of Nigerians. This is what this book is all about.

Nigerian development from 1960 was no doubt very rapid. The development was no doubt circumscribed on the structural alone. The development is yet to be essential, fundamental and complete because it lacks proper consideration to the peoples' socioeconomic, cultural and ethnic cleavage and sense of belonging. It failed to oblige the value of Nigerians; the hard-working spirit, talents and variety and diversity; rich in human resources and unite as one indivisible citizen.

Proper knowledge of the past (history) must break walls of division, counter spurious competition, face genuine geographical division of labor among the regions with dynamics of comparative advantage and decongest central crises.

Given the fact that Nigerian development begun with vicissitude of economic, political, ethnic and class struggles like many countries; it needs more than focus on political structure at the cost of its fundamental development. At the beginning of the Nigerian conflict was a kind of stratified and un-stratified struggle which includes violence, hostility, wars over resources, indirect violence causing hunger, sickness and starvation, withholding economic investment and capital and causing unemployment, unsafe and poor working environment, economic pressure and intimidation, cheap labor, lobbying, bribery and corruption and assassination. Such was the un-stratified form of Nigerian early struggles. The stratified struggle was perhaps on other levels for instance education and status quo. Only the rich could reach education. Education was seen as the emancipation from physical slavery alone and it was the heritage of the rich. The benefits from education were meant to belong to the top class of the citizens as an honor; little was it known that education is necessary for its contribution and for the emancipation of the mind, concept, will and the emotion for a just action and in building a just and fair society. Such was the backdrops of the rapid development on which Nigerian self rule and development was founded. There is need for the Nigerian leadership to properly acknowledge the past mistakes, demonstrate understanding of it, come up with inspired priority and proper motivation of the people and build a lasting social unity out of the past with the present in favor of the future for a greater sociopolitical change. Any person who learns from the past often belongs to the best.

The four corners of Nigeria present no argument about where the East, West, North or South is. The East is the direction in which sun rises, or the direction that lies directly ahead of the person facing the rising sun. The East lies opposite West. Regions that are situated toward the east are regarded as lying within East. North is the direction that lies directly to the left of the person facing the rising Sun. South is direction toward the right facing the rising Sun. People have inhabited these places before the dawn of amalgamation.

People cannot walk away from their history but they can "rewrite" it by adapting in positive ways. Individuals are inseparable from their history but they can shape it. Political practices are of course related to events that happened in the past and as well shapes the future. People in the course of political practices learn to refrain from abusing history for political profit and for future reasons. Some people although learned to abuse history in the course of political practices; given the second chance they would love to do it differently looking at the impact of their mistakes on people and on the environment. History and

The knowledge of history play essential role in every set of political leadership and exercise. It determines to a high proportion the level of accountability of the leadership behavior; it opens vista of insights and keener hindsight that can help to define peoples' future, abilities and vision.

E.P. Thompson claimed that "history is not simply the property of historians" and it can also be said that history is not a handmaid of story writers or story tellers. History is about the past. The meaning assigned to historical narratives is that it tells what happened, who made it happen, how it happened and why. Every history is not only about the past but must impact the future; and of course, the bitter impact of history can be avoided in the present and for the benefit of the future; this is what this book can say about Nigeria.

The meaning and impact of Nigerian history did not take for granted that mere politically minded actors may thwart the "subject matter of history", and make history a subject matter of politics and end up making politics a competitive game of the famous and the strong. It makes politics an agora of the strong and the famous. It would end up making the classroom empty because there would be nothing to learn; and it would bring about lack of teachers because there will be nothing to teach. Has Nigeria a history? If she does, then teach it. If Nigeria has a history then make it part of the educational and academic curriculum if you want to modify and modernize Nigeria.

E.H. Carr, in his book "What is History?" wrote that historical truths lie somewhere between valueless facts and value judgments. He argued that those political actors play on the minds of people. They downplay objective facts. They merely interpret history subjectively and refuse to see what is objective about history.

Norman Davies mentioned Carr's work in his interview commending that there is need to separate evidence of history from judgment from history. Historical wisdom should help us infer a leader and explain the present and predict the future.

Richard Evans argues on the need that the society should be able to attain the kind of objective certainty about the great issues of the time in appreciating the disposition of historical truths that can serve as a reliable basis for taking vital decisions for peoples' future in the twenty-first century. History helps to explain the world and motivates people to take action that changes the future. Many politicians including Nigerian politicians have used a partisan view of history to further their own ends.[1]

Howard Zinn argues on the biases of partisan actors in his book. He argues that historians employ a double-standard with regard to covering history and that partisan actors basically serve a propagandistic role in the society. Politicians should be good

---

[1] Politics of the Past: The Use and Abuse of Historyby Hannes Swoboda and Jan Marinus Wiersma

historians and should not be charlatans but must participate in true social change. There is hindsight in historical facts.

Accurate interpretation and proper knowledge of history must contribute to reduce agitations, unnecessary struggles and insensitivity; bigotry, ethnic and racial strife, inequality and feelings of superiority, injustice, and nationalistic fervor; knowledge is the source of rapid development and strong foundation.

Politics and Religion

When it comes to issues relating to the relationship between politics and religion in Nigeria, what the matter requests is the analysis of religion, its impact and the most pragmatic ways it leads people towards finding greater solution to life and living together in the most harmonious way in a political setting. Anything outside this is divisive. This is the only way religion becomes indispensably relevant to society.

Any society that impugns religious truth concerning building an enduring society has everything but true foundation.

Where it comes to pragmatic politics; politicians are aware that political viewpoints and actions will not endure for too long unless it avails of not only practical ways of reaching solution to human struggles using critical thinking but as well as based on religious ethical concept. Only on this that religion and politics can work together for the survival of the Nigerian society.

Politics is not just about pushing partisan platform agenda. What partisan political agenda means for a society of multi-cultural and multi-lingual and multi-religious and multi-ethnic dimension like Nigeria is everything than peace.

T. S. Eliot believed that democratic societies rejected the influence of an established religion at their peril, for in doing so they cut themselves off from the kind of ethical wisdom that can come only from participation in a tradition. As a result, he argued, such a society would degenerate into tyranny and/or social and cultural fragmentation.

Scruton offered that the healthy *polis* requires a substantial amount of pre- or extra-political social cohesion. More specifically, a certain amount of social cohesion is necessary both to ensure that citizens see themselves as sufficiently connected to each other (so that they will want to cooperate politically), and to ensure that they have a common framework within which they can make coherent collective political decisions. And I believe that social cohesion in turn is dependent on a substantial amount of self-belonging; especially with respect to adherence to certain values.

Within the period of thirty-nine years, 1960-1999, the Nigerian military ruled the country for twenty-nine years in a series of coups and counter coup. These coups brought one military government to replace another. These replacements did not convince anyone that the military was sincere to hand over power to the civilians, even when some military governments promised or began the process of transition. General Aguiyi Ironsi government promised but was not even allowed to draw up a transition program before it was overthrown. Another military, Gowon, promised to hand over government but later postponed indefinitely the transition program. This shows lack of commitment and insincerity. Murtala Mohammed learnt a big lesson from Gowon's failure. He overthrew Gowon and started in earnest the process of transition, but again the Nigerian military over threw him and punctuated the transition. A person who learns from the past would not be anything than the best. Obasanjo learned so many lessons from all of these past and pursued with vigor his transition program and handed over to a civil rule even though he was not sure about how long transition would prevail. Again, the military over threw the Shagari government. Buhari did not commit himself to hand over power before Babangida over threw him. Babangida tried to transform into civilian president. His attempt failed. Abacha was not foresighted enough he tried also to transform into civilian president but could not. He could not read the writing on the wall. After pushing out Shonekan; his attempt to transform into a civilian president was brought to an end by death. Abdulsalami like Obasanjo got the lesson and in his determination to prevent another coup, quickly proceeded with handover to civilian which brought into power Chief Olusegun Obasanjo as a civilian president under PDP. Bravo to Obasanjo and Abdulsalami. Thus, circumstances or sincerity compelled Obasanjo and Abdulsalami to hand over power in 1979 and 1999 respectively. (Cf. Victor Semawon Akrani).

The Prestige of a Nation

Nigeria needs a leader who is educated, intelligent and visionary. The world acclamation of a Nigerian leader happened at a time in July 25-28 1961 a Nigerian Prime Minister visited the United States of America. He had one of the greatest reception American government has given to any foreign black leader. Sir Abubakar Tafawa Balewa was offered honorary citizenship in three states in United States of America. The respect and dignity his visit to America accords Nigerians is unimaginable. Sir Abubakar Tafawa Balewa was called to address the US House of Representative. He spoke few words on freedom, liberty and democracy and promised the world that never will the light of creative and initiative freedom, altruistic liberty and patriotic democracy dim or weaken in Nigeria.

The survival of a nation's economy lies on how much trust foreign investors have with the country that would move them to establish in the country. The prestige of a nation is based on how much their product is worth in the world market and this speaks in an undertone the value placed on their education in the world circle. A nation's prestige is also challenged by the contribution of their intellectual to the world circle. Prestige is also challenged by the stability of the nation's economy. The political condition of a nation contributes greatly on the stability of the country's economy.

How the citizens of the country love their country and are willing to work together toward the greatness of their country contributes in the prestige of the country. The prospect and prestige of a country can be measured by the vision of their past leaders, present and future.

CHAPTER 1

COMMENTARY ON THE CHRONOLOGY OF NIGERIAN HISTORY

THE SCRAMBLE FOR WEST AFRICA

About 300 years of slave trade competition happened in Africa. The company names the Royal Adventurers later transformed to the Royal African Company along with other European monopoly companies held stocks for slave trade and other business activities. Towards 1700s Britain and France had out-competed the Dutch in the trade on West Africa. Towards 1799-1815 the end of the French Revolution followed by the Napoleonic Wars Britain had out-classed the French and dominated trade around West Africa. Britain had become the dominant commercial power in West Africa. Slave trade happened for three centuries and was the central trade conflict between the European merchants. Britain because of the increasing abolitionist intervention changed and opened new market role in the nineteenth century trading on agriculture and manufactured goods like palm oil, cocoa, palm carnel, ivory etc, and eventually took dominion of the territory on what they later named Nigeria. British formally claimed the territory called Nigeria in 1861 and began to administer Lagos as a crown colony. This was the means to protect the already illegal slave trade happening and to forestall the French from finding reason to infiltrate into the territory. Britain already had great advantage on the territory by 1906.

The British Trade

It is believable that the British merchants had scouted the territory for the past three hundred years before 1800s. The part of West Africa which was later named Nigeria falls within the territory which Britain claimed. Towards 1880 the wave and network of slave trade which begun early or before 1600 was subsiding. The British merely changed the brand name or the business name called slave trade to international trade by virtue of which it is possible to claim the territory for further exploration and exploitation and to win over other international bodies that might wish to compete on the same territory.

The Royal Niger Company

The Royal Niger Company had extended trading activities toward the hinterland in the Niger area. In 1885, British claims to a West African sphere of influence received international recognition from other prospective competitors and in the following year, the Royal Niger Company was chartered under the leadership of Sir George Taubman Goldie.

The British Government

In 1900, the company's territory came under the control of the British Government, which moved to strengthen its hold over the Niger area of the present day Nigeria. On 1 January 1901, Nigeria became a British protectorate which makes it part of the British Empire, Great Britain the foremost world power.

The Name "Nigeria"

There was a British woman called Flora Louise Shaw who later was known and called Lady Lugard; she was a British journalist and writer. Her live spanned from December 19 1852 to January 25 1929, she lived for 77 years of age. She was credited with having coined the name "Nigeria".

She wrote an essay which first appeared in *The Times* on January 8 1897, in which she suggested the name "Nigeria" for the British Protectorate on the Niger River. In that essay, Miss

Shaw wrote a short script about a number of people which was later used in the merging of a group of people as states which officially replaced the title; the "Royal Niger Company Territories".

According to her "Royal Niger Company Territories" was a very long sentence to be used as a name of a place. She coined a new name hence she came out with the coinage "Nigeria" from "Niger area".[2] The two words came together to make one name.

Shaw was married on June 10 1902 to Lugard, who, in 1928 was Baron Lugard. She accompanied him when he served as Governor of Hong Kong (1907–1912) and Governor-General of Nigeria (1914–1919).

In 1905, Shaw wrote a script that defines and stood for history of Western Sudan and the modern settlement of Northern Nigeria, which is *a purview of the history of the Western Soudan*

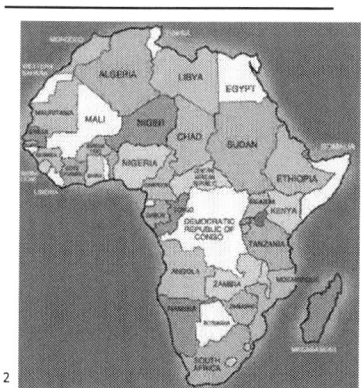

2

and at the same time cast light on the modern settlement of Northern Nigeria.

The Amalgamation

In 1914, the area formally called the Royal Niger Company Territory was formally united by amalgamation[3] as the Colony and Protectorate of Nigeria. By way of administration Nigeria continues with its division into the Northern and Southern Provinces and Lagos Colony.

Southern Nigeria was more open to the Western education and influence than the North. The focus of the Nigerian elites was more on the structural development following modernized economy and Westernized political programs which apparently proceeded more rapidly while the foundation and essence of the

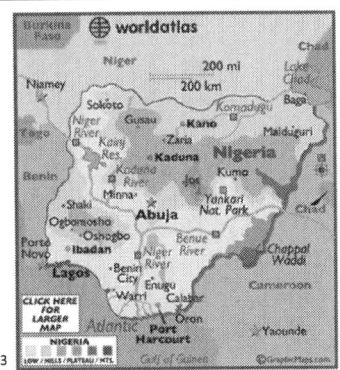
3

modern political states was very shallow. The impacts of these shallow influences were felt more on the Nigerian political actors. The British Imperial political category was a developed schema of political order which reflected the high standard of British past and potential goals and posterity. The Nigerian political actors were shallow and charlatans and did not learn this.

BRITISH FEDERALIZED NIGERIA

Due to the World War I & II influence on world affairs there was rapid growth of spirit of nationalism and patriotism in every part of the world. Nigeria was not isolated though still under British rule and being in the process of self-rule Nigeria had the impact of these waves of world crises as a primary factor. Secondly by the preceding of implementation of different kinds of try-out constitutions legislated by the British Government in preparation of the ground for Nigeria to attain self-government through representative and federal system of government and considering the fact of its multi-cultural and hetero religious and diversity needs; British considered autonomy even to the minority ethnic groups in Nigerian divers situation to federalize the country as the best option. Federalizing Nigeria in consideration of its diversity and autonomy to the minority ethnic groups was in the original project of the British.

Nigeria, is a country in West Africa, it has border with Niger in the north. It has Chad in the northeast. It has Cameroon in the east and Benin in the west. Its coast in the south is located on the Gulf of Guinea in the Atlantic Ocean.

On October 1 1954, the colony became the autonomous Federation of Nigeria. By the middle of the 20th century, the great wave for independence was sweeping across Africa. On 27 October 1958 Britain agreed that Nigeria would become an independent state on October 1 1960. Nigeria attained her independence and federation on October 1 1960 under a constitution that provided for a parliamentary[4] government and a substantial measure of self-government for the country's three regions.

46 Years after Amalgamation

On January 1, 1914, Lord Frederick Lugard, the governor of both the Northern Nigeria Protectorate and the Colony and Protectorate of Southern Nigeria, signed a document consolidating and amalgamating the two territories, thereby creating the Colony and Protectorate of Nigeria. Forty-six years later in 1960, Nigeria became an independent state.

THE NIGERIAN SELF-RULE

---

[4] *"A parliamentary form of government is a democratic one where the head of state and head of government are held by different people and the executive and legislative branches of government are linked.* The executive and legislative branches are linked because the executive branch gets its power from the legislative branch and is held accountable for their actions by them as well"

From 1959 to 1960, Jaja Nwachuku was the First Nigerian Speaker of the Nigerian Parliament, also called the "House of Representatives." Jaja Nwachuku replaced Sir Frederick Metcalfe of Britain. Notably, as First Speaker of the House,

The Document of Self-rule

The Self-rule Charter gives exclusive powers in the followings:

Defense; this means that the country can recruit her police and army or any other security organization found relevant to attain the country's political and security objectives.

Foreign Relations; the country can engaged in trade, sports, culture, diplomatic etc., in conformity with rules and regulation with other countries in accordance with international law.

Commercial and Fiscal Policy; that the country has power to make policies following her trade, professional matters, monetary and economic issue etc.

Governance and Political Affairs; that the country has the political sovereignty to adopt any leadership method to govern her citizens.

Jaja Nwachuku received Nigeria's Instrument of Independence, also known as Freedom Charter, on 1 October 1960, from Princess Alexandra of Kent, The Queen's representative at the Nigerian first independence ceremonies.

The Federal government was given exclusive powers in defense, foreign relations, and commercial and fiscal policy.

---

[5] The legislative branch in a bicameral legislature (parliament)

"In a unicameral parliament all members of parliament sit in the same chamber and vote on major policy decisions. In a bicameral parliament members meet and vote in two separate chambers, usually called the lower house and upper house. *Bicameral system*, also called *bicameralism*, a system of government in which the legislature comprises two houses. The modern bicameral system dates back to the beginnings of constitutional government in 17th-century England and to the later 18th century on the continent of Europe and in the United States."

Legislative power was vested in a bicameral parliament,[5] executive power in a prime minister and cabinet and judicial authority in a Federal Supreme Court.

Political parties, however, tended to reflect the makeup of the three main ethnic groups in Nigeria. The Nigerian People's Congress (NPC) represented conservative, Muslim, largely Hausa and Fulani interests that dominated the Northern Region. The northern region of the country consists of three-quarters of the land area and more than half the population of Nigeria. Thus the North dominated the federation government from the beginning of independence. (Cf. the map of Nigeria in the lower page of this book).

THE NIGERIAN LEADERSHIP APPROACH

Partisan conflict, faction, ethnic biases, rigging elections and other forms of public embarrassment were the findings which seriously hinder the smooth history of the development of the Nigerian leadership approach. This apparently to a certain degree is suggestive of the absence of individual and common political will that is capable of imagining and envisioning the preference of the future. These approaches certainly deserve proper evaluation if the present day leadership would make learning experience out of that and attain constructive reform.

The First Nigerian Election of 1959			
Party	Vote	Percentile	Seats
National Council of Nigeria and the Cameroons†	2,594,577	34.0	81
Action Group	1,992,364	26.1	73
Northern Peoples' Congress	1,922,179	25.2	134
Northern Elements Progressive Union	509,050	6.7	8
Mabolaje Grand Alliance			6
Igala Union			4
Independence	610,677	8.0	2
Igbira Tribal Union			1
Niger Delta Congress			1
Total	7,628,847	100	312

In the 1959 elections held in preparation for independence, the NPC got 134 seats in the 312-seat parliament, leaving 178 seats for the remaining eight groups.

NCNC got 89 seats in the federal parliament as the second largest party in the newly independent country the National Council of Nigerian Citizens NCNC which represented the interests of the Igbo- and Christian-dominated people of the Eastern Region of Nigeria; while the Action Group (AG) was a left-leaning party that represented the interests of the Yoruba people in the West obtained 73 seats and the remaining seats were taken up as indicated on the table below.

The first post-independence national government was formed by a conservative alliance of the NCNC and the NPC. It was widely suspected and expected that Ahmadu Bello the Sardauna of Sokoto, one of the strongest influence in Nigeria who controlled the North, would become Prime Minister of the new federation of the Nigerian government. But he defiled the predicted, and rather chose to remain as premier of the North and as party leader of the NPC, selected Sir Abubakar Tafawa Balewa to become Nigeria's first Prime Minister.

AG was dominated by the Yoruba and following the political situation became the opposition under its radical leader Chief Obafemi Awolowo.

The Beginning of Political Faction in the West

No sooner had the independence been celebrated in 1960 than faction erupted in 1962 within the AG under the leadership of Ladoke Akintola who had been selected as Premier of the West. The Akintola faction argued that the Yoruba people were losing their substantial position in business affairs in Nigeria to people of the Igbo tribe because the Igbo-dominated NCNC was part of the governing coalition and the AG was not.

The Prime Minister, Balewa considered the Akintola faction and made the AG join the government.

The party leadership under Awolowo refused to accept that and replaced Akintola as premier of the West with one of their own supporters. When Western Region parliament met to approve this change, Akintola supporters in the parliament staged a riot in the chambers of the parliament and physical fighting between the members broke out and chairs were used against one person and another and one of the members got hold of the Parliamentary Mace and was using it to attack others along with the Speaker of the House before the police fired tear gas which caused everyone to flee. The riot continued even in the subsequent attempts to reconvene the Western Parliament including rigged elections.

Consequently, the Prime Minister Tafawa Balewa declared martial law in the Western Region and arrested Awolowo and other members of his faction and charged them for treasonable offense.

Akintola was appointed to head a coalition government in the Western Region which projected the AG rather as doing an opposition role in their own territory.

The Sudden End of the Parliamentary Government

Shortly the parliamentary system of government ended as a result of leadership squabbles, power struggle and political factions giving way to the federal system of government, which was termed the "Federal Republic".

Nigerian First Federal Republic

Right from the beginning Nigerian political and class struggles, tribal, ethnic and religious tensions were resonated by the disparities in economic and educational development and ethnic attachment between the South and the North. The South had more Westernized elites but the North was more organized and united.

In October 1963 Nigeria proclaimed itself the Federal Republic of Nigeria, and former Governor General Nnamdi Azikiwe became the country's first President.

The AG lost control of the Western Region in the feeling that the Federal Government had maneuvered against them and a new pro-government Yoruba party, the Nigerian National Democratic Party (NNDP), took over shortly afterward and the AG opposition leader, Chief Obafemi Awolowo, was imprisoned.

The 1965 national election produced incredible election malpractices and a disputed result that set the country on the path to civil war.

The Second Political Faction in the West

The dominant northern NPC went into a conservative alliance with the new Yoruba NNDP, leaving the Igbo NCNC to coalesce with the remnants of the AG in a progressive alliance.

There was a resounding electoral fraud in the vote. Riots erupted in the Yoruba West where the AG discovered they had apparently elected pro-government NNDP representatives.

The Sudden End of the First Federal Republic

What was known as the federal republic survived not more than three years and turned out to be chaos, fraud, corruption and electoral malpractices, religious and tribal conflict; the first federal republic was defunct and gave way for the military juntas.

(THE SIMMERING OF THE NIGERIAN CIVIL WAR)

The Chaos of the First Military Rule and First Unsuccessful Coup

15 January 1966 was a very sad day when a number of young army majors and military juntas mostly from the south-eastern Nigeria overthrew the NPC-NNDP government and assassinated the Prime Minister and the Premiers of the Northern and Western regions.

Even though the coup was deadly, bloody and fearsome it failed to achieve its goal of taking over the government and rid the country of corruption; consequently causing another coup to be carried out and installing General Johnson Aguiyi Ironsi as the Head of State.

Major Emmanuel Ifeajuna fled to Ghana-Kwame Nkrumah's government and others went into hiding. Some of the Young Majors were arrested and detained by the Ironsi government.

In the Northern Region, the Hausa and Fulani people however believed that the coup was an Igbo coup against the north and demanded that the detainees be placed on trial for murder.

With the look of things, some people were dissatisfied with the Federal Military Government that assumed power under General Johnson Aguiyi Ironsi which seems unable to control ethnic tensions and series of agitation.

Moreover, the Ironsi government was unable to produce a constitution that is acceptable to all sections of the country.

Most acceptable for the Ironsi government was the decision to issue Decree No. 34 which sought to unify the nation as unitary system of government.

Decree No. 34 sought to do away with the whole federal structure under which the Nigerian government had been organized since independence.

Sequel to that a demonstration started in Zaria by the students of the Institute of Administration and also the Ahmadu Bellow University against the unification decree No. 34 which they were not amenable to.

The students were uncomfortable because they sensed that the decree might disfavor their self claim rights towards northern "exclusive workforce". And may adversely throw the north open for competition for jobs and they might lose the relatively exclusive job market of the north to southern counterparts and rivals.

The Reason for the First and Second Military Coup

The first military coup that failed was embarked on by the said Young Majors as a result of the following reasons:

- Corruption from the leaders

- Lack of real political aim on the governing authorities

- Electoral malpractices and conflicts

- Division within the political classes

- Politicians' selfish interest

- Disproportionate gap between the elites-rich and the masses (Cf. Adewale Ademoyega 1981 "Why we Struck").

According to Adewale one of the three Majors who incited and led the first Nigerian coup of 1966 in his aim to clarify that the coup had no ethnic biases as most Hausas and Fulanis believed and to debunk peoples' perception of the coup as an

Igbo coup gave the following reasons: first was that the plot was hatched among other army officers and led by the three Majors: Kaduna Nzeogwu, Emmanuel Ifeajuna and Adewale Ademoyega. Second reason was that it was General Aguiyi Ironsi who intercepted and fought to foil the plot. So it is reasonable enough to overcome the temptation of believing that it was an Igbo coup. Common sense exercise may help anyone to arrive that the plot was not an Igbo plot. The third reason was that the names short-listed to be arrested, four of which were from the north, two were from the west and two were from the east. (Cf. the Book "Why we Struck").

The following names of civilians, military and police were those who died as a result of the 1966 coup plot:

Civilians:

- Prime Minister Abubakar Tafawa Balewa
- Premier Ahmadu Bello
- Premier Samuel Ladoke Akintola

- Finance Minister Festus Okotie-Eboh

- Ahmed Ben Musa (Senior Assistant Secretary for Security)

- Hafsatu Bello

- Mrs Latifat Ademulegun

- Zarumi Sardauna

- Ahmed Pategi, (Government driver)

- Minister of Finance (Fetus Okotie Eboh)

Military and police:

- Brig. Samuel Ademulegun

- Brig. Zakariya Maimalari

- Col. Ralph Shodeinde

- Col. Kur Mohammed

- Lt. Col. Abogo Largema

- Lt. Col. James Pam

- Lt. Col. Arthur Unegbe

- Sergeant Daramola Oyegoke (assisted Nzeogwu in the attack on the Sardauna's lodge and according to the Police report was murdered by Nzeogwu)
- PC Yohana Garkawa
- Lance Corporal Musa Nimzo
- PC Akpan Anduka
- PC Hagai Lai
- Philip Lewande

The second military coup was successful because there was a military take over. At the same time there was found to be leadership flaws and aimless because it could not quell the tension and social upheaval in the country. It gave way to another military coup and bloody confrontations again.

The Chaos of the Third Military Coup and the Civil War

For the reasons that brought the military government of Ironsi to power and the abolishment of the federal system of government and renamed the country "the Republic of Nigeria on 24 May 1966; riots was staged in the north. This led to another coup planned and carried out by the northern army officers in July 1966 and installed Major General Yakubu Gowon as the Head of State.

The name Federal Republic of Nigeria was restored on 31 August 1966. However, the subsequent killings of thousands of Igbo people in the North triggered a massive return to the Igbo land by the Igbo people.

CHAPTER 2

THE HAPHAZARD FEDERALIST STYLE OF NIGERIAN GOVERRNMENT

This book predicates haphazard to The Nigerian federal style of governance because there seems to be absence of plan longitudinally followed by each government or the subsequent government that depicts the modern federalist model. The approach each government gave was somewhat hazy; which was the reason that the country remained stagnant and after sixty years of independence the only tangible improvement that the Nigerian environment could celebrate is the use of mobile communication and internet. The country needs electric train and easy transportation means from one state to another, security policies that can stabilize the economy and energy stability and to give substantial autonomy to the states so that every hard-working states may become the trailblazer for modern standard of living while others would try to imitate them. That is how fast to make the country grow. The haphazard federalism was exacerbated by a long span of military power.

THE INDIRECT RULE SYSTEM

The map of modern Nigeria was drawn with the amalgamation in 1914 which becomes the basis for political references. The merging of the Northern and Southern region by the British in order to exert indirect rule system which already was successful in the Northern region was a method and model of leadership which employed the initiative and influence of the local authorities. The Colonial Governor Frederick Lugard thought diplomatically on the success and unity of his administration for both the North and the South using indirect rule hence the amalgamation of both regions would for him make it easy for indirect rule to thrive. So amalgamation was Frederick Lurgard's tool for indirect rule whereby a foreign system of governance may be imposed on the newly merged protectorates.

By 1940s there were already the Igbo and Yoruba groups putting pressure on the British demanding for independence. Towards 1950s the Igbo groups of intellectuals began to increase in number and to agitate for nondiscriminatory rights and for self-rule.

As for the Northern people the indirect rule of the British was to be allowed based on the hypotheses that self-rule may not warrant fair economic and political judgment thereby opening a floodgate of discrimination and dominion by the Southerners who have acquired more Western influence through education. Afraid of the increasing number of the Southern Westernized Elites the Northern leaders showed reluctance in fighting the British rule for independence rather would prefer that the Colonial governance continue. The indirect rule system was the seed-bed where the substantial autonomy for each region was nursed and hatched by the federalized Nigeria.

AUTONOMY AS YAKUBU GOWAN'S REASON FOR THE 12 STATES DIVISION

Major General Yakubu Gowon envisaged autonomy of the regional states from the federal government as a solution in order to quell the turbulence in the Nigerian politics. General Gowon moved towards greater autonomy to minority ethnic groups and began to initiate the federalist model that would protect autonomy of the states. This was the direct or indirect primary cause for the British choice of indirect rule to be later transformed into federation for the Nigerian diverse nature in order to accommodate the country's multi-ethnic nature.

Any right thinking person will sense such hindsight as an element which distinguished Gowon's regime from other Nigerian Military regimes and led General Gowon to split the four regions into 12 states.[6] It was saddening that Gowon

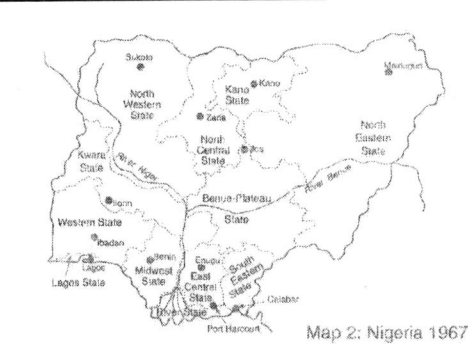

Map 2: Nigeria 1967

6

afterwards got involved in power temptation and lost his "vision" and could not perfect his hindsight.

Autonomy in the popular English dictionary means the right and fundamental condition following self-government. And in Kantian moral philosophy autonomy means; the ability of a moral agent to act in conformity with objective morality (right and correct) as opposed to acting under the prejudice or influence of desires (emotion, passion). Modern federalist nations are progressive because the local states are autonomous from the central government:

> "Federalism is the theory or advocacy of federal principles for dividing powers between member units and common institutions. Unlike in a unitary state, sovereignty in federal political orders is non-centralized, often constitutionally, between at least two levels so that units at each level have final authority and can be self governing in some issue area. Citizens thus have political obligations to, or have their rights secured by, two authorities. The division of power between the member unit and center may vary, typically the center has powers regarding defense and foreign policy, but member units may also have international roles. The decision-making bodies of member units may also participate in central decision-making

bodies. Much recent philosophical attention is spurred by renewed political interest in federalism and backlashes against particular instances, coupled with empirical findings concerning the requisite and legitimate basis for stability and trust among citizens in federal political orders. Philosophical contributions have addressed the dilemmas and opportunities facing Canada, Australia, Europe, Russia, Iraq, Nepal and Nigeria, to mention just a few areas where <u>federal arrangements</u> are seen as interesting solutions to accommodate differences <u>among populations divided by ethnic or cultural cleavages</u> yet seeking common, often democratic, political order." (Cf. Stanford Encyclopedia of Philosophy Revised June 7 2018).

What does the name Federal Republic of Nigeria Insinuate? With what aim in mind was the country restored to the Federal Republic as the best system of government for Nigeria if not for the diverse ethnic, cultural and social and population cleavage? What are the most significant factors considered aside from the diverse ethnic nature?

The Central Intelligence Agency commented in October 1966 in a CIA Intelligence Memorandum that:

"Africa's most populous country (population estimated at 48 million) is in the throes of a highly complex internal crisis rooted in its artificial origin as a British dependency containing over 250 diverse and often antagonistic tribal groups".

The CIA went forward in the comment stating what purport to be the cause of the problem:

> "The present crisis started" with Nigerian independence in 1960, but the federated parliament hid "serious internal strains. It has been in an acute stage since last January when a military coup d'état destroyed the constitutional regime bequeathed by the British and upset the underlying tribal and regional power relationships".

From such situation the CIA predicted the impossibility of the country surviving as one unitary state when it says:

> The most fundamental questions which can be raised about Nigeria is whether it will survive as a single viable entity. The country has less chance of reaching stability under one unitary and central government. Unless there is a new agreement; security situation will continue to deteriorate and possibly a civil war may set in". (Cf. CIA Memorandum 1 October 1966).

Soon after the CIA prediction it was the Aburi Conference where the Nigerian leaders sought counsel for the settlement of the deteriorating condition of the country.

GOWON AND OJUKWU AND THE ABURI MEETING

According to Rtd. Lt. Col. Emeka Odumegwu Ojukwu in an interview, there was no mention of the word "confederation" in the meeting at Aburi. According to Rtd. Major General Yakubu Gowon in an interview, "I was down with fever when I arrived from Aburi meeting I could not announce the outcome of the meeting and Ojukwu did not wait for me to announce the outcome. He chose to announce to the Igbo people the outcome of the Aburi meeting and that was my resentment against him". This account insinuate emotional than intentional action on the part of Gowon. Gowon lacks the freedom to act with objective correctness based on the outcome of Aburi conference. He showed one of the highest irresponsibility in the leadership that set Nigeria backward. If he were a true leader he would take full responsibility of the "Aburi Charter".

What was Agreed Upon in Aburi Meeting?

Information available showed that so many things were said on the conference on January 4 and 5 1967. But the most important of them was topics agreed upon that have consequences and implications on the Nigerian future such as:

(1) To avert the imminent civil war

(2) To reorganize the armed forces for fair distribution across the four regions

(3) To review the constitution on the areas it bestowed absolute powers to the central government.

Ojukwu initiated the moves for diplomatic negotiations as it was captured on the Daily Times of Tuesday, 2nd August 1966 in his speech in the Eastern region; according to him such diplomatic responsibility and negotiation would offer Nigerians the opportunity to understand the kind of future system of government they may want to have. (Cf. Eric Teniola).

Others who Attended the Aburi Meeting

The Chairman of the Ghana National Liberation Council, Lt-General J.A. Ankrah, was the chairman and by virtue of that declared the meeting open in his capacity as the then head of state of Ghana.

Lt. Col. Yakubu Gowon, Colonel Robert Adebayo, Lt-Col. Odumegwu Ojukwu, Lt-Col David Ejoor, Lt-Col David Hassan Katsina, Commodore J.E.A. Wey, Major Mobolaji Johnson, Alhaji Kam Selem and Mr. J. Omo-Bare. Others were Prince S.I.A. Akenzua (Permanent Under-Secretary, Federal Cabinet Office.), Mr. P.T. Odumosu (Secretary to the Military Government, West.), Mr. N.U. Akpan (Secretary to the Military Government, East.), Mr. D.P. Lawani (Under-Secretary, Military Governor's Office, Mid-West) and Alhaji Ali Akilu (Secretary to the Military Government, North.)

The Detailed Charter of Aburi

It was discussed that the Army to be governed by the Supreme Military Council under a Chairman to be known as Commander-in-Chief of the Armed Forces and Head of the Federal Military Government. The Establishment of a Military Headquarters comprising equal representation from the Regions and headed by a Chief of Staff. The Creation of Area commands corresponding to existing Regions and under the charge of Area Commanders. On matters of policy, including appointments and promotion to top executive posts in the Armed Forces and the Police to be dealt with by the Supreme Military Council.

During the period of the military government, military governors will have control over area commands for internal security, creation of a Lagos Garrison including Ikeja Barracks. Concerning the re-organization of the Army, the Council agreed that the distribution of military personnel with particular reference to the present recruitment drive.

The Council agreed that general recruitment throughout the country in the present situation would cause great imbalance in the distribution of soldiers. After a lengthy discussion of the subjects, the Council agreed to set up a military committee in which each region will be represented, to prepare statistics which will show: present strength of Nigerian Army; deficiency in each sector of each unit; the size appropriate for the country and each area command; additional requirement for the country and each area command.

A committee was constituted to meet and report to the Council within two weeks from the date of receipt of instructions.

The Council agreed that pending completion of the exercise in connection with re-organization of the army, further recruitment of soldiers should cease. The implementation of the agreement reached on August 9, 1966, it was agreed, after a lengthy discussion, that it was necessary for the agreement reached on August 9 by the delegates of the regional governments to be fully implemented. In particular, it was accepted in principle that army personnel of Northern origin should return to the North from the West. It was therefore felt that a crash program of recruitment and training, the details of which would be further examined after the committee to look into the strength and distribution of army personnel had reported, would be necessary to constitute indigenous army personnel in the West to a majority there quickly. As far as the regions were concerned, it was decided that all the powers vested by the Nigerian Constitution in the regions and which they exercised prior to January 15, 1966, should be restored to the regions. To this end, the Supreme Military Council decided that all decrees passed since the military take-over, and which tended to detract from the previous powers of the regions, should be repealed by January 21, 1967, after the Law Officers should have met on January 14, 1967, to list out all such decrees.

Faction Against Aburi

It was known that Prince Akenzua along with top Permanent Secretaries including Alhaji Yusuf Gobir, Phillip Asiodu, Ime Ebong, B.N. Okagbue and Allison Ayida sat in Lagos and politically analyzed all that was agreed upon in Aburi and criticized Yakubu Gowon for swallowing hook and sinker all that was said. As a result Gowon mandated Prince Akenzua to prepare a memo forthwith to cancel Aburi agreement. The memo was dated 8th January 1967 reads:

"Your Excellency, in view of my discussion with you last night, I am raising this memo in the interest of our fatherland Nigeria".

Akenzua embellished his memo with traces of Nigeria rough past routes and expressed his embellishment with love for "United Nigeria". His Memo analyzed that Gowon had compromised so much in Aburi as to give opportunity for the break apart of the country in future through legalized total regionalism. In his assessment the whole agreement will lead to a weak central government and a confederacy; which he considered destructive for the then military government.

Based on the political analyses of the Aburi agreement and the Prince Akenzua's memo Gowon convened a sub-Aburi meeting in Benin City on 16 through 18 February 1967 with the Secretaries to the Military Government and many top office holders. The meeting was presided over by Mr. H. A. Ejueyitchie, the Secretary to the Federal Military Government.

It was on the Benin-sub-Aburi meeting where all about Aburi Accord was rejected after having politically torn apart the concord.

The Outcome of Aburi Rejection

The Federal Government headed by Lt. Col. Yakubu Gowan promulgated <u>Decree No. 8 of 1967 which gave total powers to the Central Government</u>. The implications of Decree No. 8 which was promulgated on March 10, 1967 changed the political, cultural and social landscape of Nigeria.

"On Aburi I Stand"

"On Aburi I stand" was a phrase originated from Ojukwu consequent upon the non-implementation of the Aburi Concord.

On February 16, 1967, Colonel Ojukwu wrote a letter to Gowon. In the letter he said:

> "At Aburi, certain decisions were taken by the Supreme Military Council – the highest authority of the land under that regime. For my part, I became dedicated to those decisions, only to discover soon that you and your Civil Service advisers, along with selfish and disgruntled politicians in Lagos, and perhaps elsewhere as well, did not feel the same. As a result you have seen to it that the

decision taken at Aburi are systematically vitiated or stalled".

Col. Robert Adeyinka Adebayo the Military Governor of Western region on 3rd May 1967 in his broadcast said:

"We tried at Aburi to find the basis for a solution but there was not enough confidence to build upon that basis. As a result, follow up action was slow and argument developed which further impaired confidence. When at last Decree No. 8 was passed by the Supreme Military Council, we could not carry the Eastern Region with us."

Why was the Meeting Held in Aburi?

Before the Aburi meeting Ojukwu and the Supreme Military Council (SMC) had series of hostile words against one another and accused one another of being the cause of the continuing agitations.

Lt. Col. Hassan Usman the Military Governor of the North even attacked Ojukwu from personal argument saying that Ojukwu was only trying to show off with his learnedness and eloquence in the use of English language as a graduate of Oxford University. And for him in his words; he saw Nigerian crises as a confrontation between "ambitious" Ojukwu and the rest of the country.

OJukwu had made it clear in words after the coup of July 29 1966 that he cannot make himself available on any meeting place where there would be Northern Military troops. Ojukwu and other Igbo people had refused to honor invitations from the SMC to attend a meeting on board in a British Naval ship and at Benin City and that made it clear that the appropriate venue for the meeting must be on a neutral ground away from the Northern Military troops hence Aburi in Ghana was chosen as the venue. Although Ojukwu was afraid of being abducted and killed by the Northern Military troops as much as other Igbo members but he waved off such premonition by his trust to Gowon from whom he had received a guarantee of safe passage to travel to Ghana.

THE DECLARATION OF SECESSION AND THE CIVIL WAR

The Killing of the Igbo people in the North, the priority of political power to the Northerners and the recruitment of soldiers and giving primacy to the North; the distribution of oil revenues with priority to the North with less consideration to the Southeastern territories where the sources of oil were located were additional factors to the rejection of the Aburi Accord.

The Nigerian oil revenue fraud was equally a concern for American Government over the corrupt practices of some members of the Nigerian government.

Critiques of Ojukwu have the opinion that Ojukwu having the knowledge of the territories and revenues made out of the oil reserves; was without hesitation in declaring secession for the southeastern territorial self-sufficiency and prosperity.

Lt Col. Emeka Ojukwu declared the Independence of the Eastern region on May 29 1967 and named it the Republic of Biafra on May 30 1967; the civil war started as a result.

THE 30 MONTHS WAR

The Nigerian Civil War or the Biafran War or the Nigerian-Biafran War of July 6 1967 – January 15 1970 can be seen as milestone that set in the events of Nigeria misconstrued history. In fact it was the war which showed the culmination in the conceitedness and deceitfulness in the mind of the early leaders of all the regions.

Comments and Interpretation of the 30 Months War

It is very important to consider the implication and significance of the Nigeria-Biafra war or the Nigerian Civil War.

> "We had observed over some 15 years before independence the difficulties which the leaders of the three major parts of the country, North, West and East, had shown in devising".[7]

The war however may imply that the early leaders did not benefit or appreciate any usefulness of the multi-ethnic diversity

---

[7] International Affairs vol.46 April 1970 No.2, Reflection on the Nigerian Civil War by Margery Perham, Published by Oxford University Press on behalf of the Royal Institute of International Affairs.

of Nigeria. This can also be interpreted that the war had connection with their misconception of the independence.

> "They should not have become independent; they were incapable of governing themselves".[8]

The diverse ethnic strength of the people came into amalgamation with Northern protectorate, Lagos Colony and Southern protectorate which was later named Eastern Nigeria. Their multi-culture, religion, language, skill and talents could not be harnessed as strength to build the nation's history as a cause of indivisibility and indissolubility.[9]

The special attributes of the people turn around and became the cause for fighting. Their blessing became the reason for their degeneration and backward history.

---

[8] The Nigerian Civil War in the International Press Published by Indiana University Press on hehalf of the Hutchins Center for African and African American Research of Harvard University: by Adepitan Bamisaiye.

[9] Constitution of the Federal Republic of Nigeria 1999, the General Provisions in Chapter 1, specifically in Section 2, Subsection 1 and 2.

"The long-running insurgency in the oil-producing Niger Delta region, in the country's south, has indirect links to the postwar settlement. By controlling revenues from the country's lucrative petroleum industry and requiring them to be shared nationwide, the federal government stripped control from local communities" (Max Siollun 2020).

Could it mean that Nigerians did not learn anything from the prejudices from the ideological frames of the colonial attitude?

"But Nigeria remains haunted by the ghosts of its civil war. It simply stopped the war without addressing its root causes. And by refusing to discuss the war's legacies, the country's rulers bred a deep, dangerous disenchantment (Max Siollun 2020).

The political arrangement of the country, the economic disparity of the country need to be harnessed rather than left to the hands of depraved leaders with corrupt and greed motivations? The North had great advantage in terms of the land mass; the West had great advantage in terms of early industrial influence and education and the East had great advantage in terms of mineral resources. Where have the British done wrongly for allowing the colony to attain a self-rule after 100 years? Or does this intransigence suggest that one hundred years of colonization was too small for self-rule? If indeed it was too small then five hundred years equally would be too little to learn lessons.

It may be because those foundation fathers of the country were not creative enough after participating with the British colonial administration and governance upon hinging the basis of the modern Nigeria from 1914 and for more than a century all that was learned by the early political leaders of Nigeria was authoritarianism, oppression and egocentrism and double standard; be they from North, West or East; civilian or military; none was able to demonstrate the exuberant impartial essence of the western and modern learning in a creative-transforming and altruistic leadership.

The impression left behind on the first political and leadership selection ended up with each of the three regions the dominant ethnic groups, the Hausa-Fulani, Yoruba, and Igbo, respectively formed political parties that were exclusively regional and biased and with ethnic supports and allegiances; this is a tension that needed to be properly resolved since the one hundred years of the British rule.

"However, many of the people argue that the political classes of the society have failed overtime to allow the blending of the many ethnic nationalities within its borders to have a sense of belonging or ownership of the state. Therefore, the call for the restructuring of the nation or collapse of the nation-state continues to be a recurring decimal in national debate" (Rantimi Jays Julius-Adeoye 2017).

THE HISTORIC SHORT-SIGHT OF YAKUBU GOWON AND EMEKA ODUMEGWU OJUKWU

Among those who got nearer to the corridor of the fast dawning history of the Nigerian polity; there were none as brilliant as Gowon and Ojukwu. Both of them came very, very close to the dawning civilization of the most populous African country but could not let the dawn happen. They had stiffed ambition to protect their ego; such that they could not forge a deal and manage the conflict, come to compromise and move forward. Both were top military officers in command and one wonders if the training and education they acquired had any influence on them such as to expose them to the critical knowledge of history. Moreover it was a crucial moment the world was passing through series of wars, economic recession and depression. They had a lot of lesson to learn: the World War I, 1914-1918, the World greatest economic recession, 1929-1930's, the United State's economic depression 1929-1930's, the global economic trouble when the New York Stock Exchange collapsed and there was biting inflation, unemployment and famine, including the world's greatest immigration problem that only began to settle around 1940's, the World War II, the American, Korean and Vietnam war 1955-1975 etc. Around the same moment some African regions have started witnessing green light of hope of self-rule and Nigeria was one of them which merely attain independence. History is asking Gowon and Ojukwu why they could not read the tiny writing on the wall of history. Why did they lack knowledge of diplomacy? Both of them were lacking in diplomatic strategy and patience in spite of their high level of training and education. From all insinuation the decision and mistake of both finally plunged the nation into armed conflict and the most devastated war. It is enough to judge that both had no leadership strategy quite like their predecessors and many of the subsequent Nigerian leaders. It was the lack of hindsight of Gowon and Ojukwu that opened the floodgate for the subsequent leaders who ripped off Nigerian economy. Gowon and Ojukwu worked fatiguely from Nigeria to Aburi-Ghana where they ate meals together from one plate as depicted in the page of the news paper and had great reunion and went back to Nigeria and continued with conflicting views even upon realizing that the most appropriate would be to go back to Aburi or find solution through another diplomatic means. There once was a

Constitutional Conference convened in 1954 in London where the NCNC argued against the proposal to enshrine in the constitution of the emerging independent Nigeria with reasons that the clause with the right of secession would not benefit the unity of the entire emerging nation with the unitary pattern of governance and that the provision for right of secession in the constitution would likely mar the structure of a unitary system of governance. This argument favored the precipitous condition which British designed for the country. History continues to ask why is it that these two gentle men could not see beyond their armed emotion. Their decision was more of emotion than intention. Does it show that both understood what it takes to lead a nation? Gowon lacks sense of justice and Ojukwu lacks down-to-earth sense of diplomacy and strategic patience. They knew too well that Nigerian ethnic conflict was nearly forty years as at the time the Biafran, Nigerian war ended; from 1930 to 1970. There is something history is not quite sure about Gowon and Ojukwu, their predecessors and subsequent leaders;

and that is; if they were to be given the second chance; that means if events were to be back-tracked; what would they like to do differently?

> "History with its flickering lamp stumbles along the trail of the past, trying to reconstruct its scenes, to revive its echoes, and kindle with pale gleams the passion of former days. What is the worth of all this? The only guide to a man is his conscience; the only shield to his memory is the rectitude and sincerity of his actions. It is very imprudent to walk through life without this shield, because we are so often mocked by the failure of our hopes and the upsetting of our calculations; but with this shield, however the fates may play, we march always in the ranks of honor."
> (Winston Churchill).

"There must be what Mr. Gladstone many years ago called a blessed act of oblivion. We must all turn our backs upon the horrors of the past. We must look to the future. We cannot afford to drag forward across the years that are to come the hatreds and revenges which have sprung from the injuries of the past." (Winston Churchill).

> "The farther backward you can look, the farther forward you are likely to see." (Winston Churchill).

THE FORTH MILITARY COUP

On 29 July 1975 in a bloodless coup d'etat the regime of General Yakubu Gowon was overthrown by Brigadier Murtala Mohammed. Brigadiar Olusegun Obasanjo was appointed the deputy to the regime of Murtala Muhammed. Gowon attended the twelfth Organization of African Unity OAU meeting in Kampala, Uganda when the coup d'etat against his regime took place. Murtala Muhammed disagreed with some of Gowon's policies and his regime offered among other reasons for the overthrow of Gowon's regime that Gowon was making less progress towards handing over power to civilian rule.

Use of Power by Murtala Mohammed

Murtala Mohammed further set the character of federalism backward; he forced a unitary model of government by hijacking the authority reserved for the states, imposing the authority of federal government in places that were reserved for the states.

He made one of his priorities efforts to reduce inflation by reducing the huge money supply.

THE FIFTH MILITTARY COUP AND SECOND UNSUCCESSFUL COUP

General Murtala Mohammed was assassinated on 13 February 1976 in an abortive coup led by Lieutenant Colonel Bukar Suka Dimka, due to the unsuccessful coup plot Murtala Mohammed's chief of staff Lt. Gen. Olusegun Obasanjo became head of state.

Lt. Gen. Olusegun Obasanjo quickly began to prepare the country for a civilian rule. A constituent assembly was elected in 1977 to draft a new constitution. The new constitution was published on 21 September 1978. The ban on political activity was lifted in 1978. In 1979, five political parties emerged and competed in a series of elections in which Alhaji Shehu Shagari of the National Party of Nigeria (NPN) was elected president. The five parties were all represented in the National

Assemble by winning the seats. By 1979 there was the oil boom in Nigeria, with Nigeria becoming the sixth largest producer of oil in the world with revenues from oil of $24 billion per year.

In August 1983 after the election Mr Shehu Shagari and the NPN were returned to power in a landslide winning majority of the seats in the National Assembly taking the control of 12 state governments. However it was noticed that the elections were full of violence and allegations of pervasive vote rigging and electoral misconduct which resulted to legal squabbles about who won the election.

THE SIXTH MILITARY COUP

On December 31, 1983, Shehu Shagari just five months into his second term; the military overthrew the second republic. Major General Muhammadu Buhari emerged as the leader of the Supreme Military Council (SMC) and the new head of the government.

THE SEVENTH MILITARY COUP

In August 27, 1985 General Ibrahim Babangida overthrew the regime of General Buhari peacefully. Babangida was the Third in rank among the SMC members. Babangida offered the following reasons that warranted his coup plot: misuse of power, violations of human rights economic crisis and the government failure to establish economic stability of the country.

During his first days in office Babangida moved to restore freedom of the press and to release political detainees being held without charge and as part of a 15-month economic emergency plan he announced pay slash for the military, police, civil servants and the private sector.

Babangida demonstrated intentions to encourage public participation in decision making by opening a national debate on proposed economic reform and recovery measures. The public response convinced Babangida of the fact that there was intense opposition towards economic recession. He accomplished The Third Mainland Bridge in Lagos which is sometimes called the

Ibrahim Babangida Boulevard which is about 11.8 kilometers which is the longest bridge connecting Lagos mainland to the Lagos Island. He utilized the ECOWAS monitoring group called ECOMOG, a military troupe that intervened in waging war and bringing peace and stability in Liberia in 1990. Babangida accomplished the plans to relocate the federal capital territory from Lagos to Abuja in 1991.

THE CHAOS OF THE THIRD UNSUCCESSFUL COUP AND EIGHTH MILITARY COUP

Babangida promised to return the country to civilian rule by 1990 which was later extended until January 1993. In early 1989 a constituent assembly completed a constitution and before the end of the first quarter of the year political activity was again permitted. In October 1989 the government established a two party political system the National Republican Convention (NRC) and the Social Democratic Party (SDP); no other parties were allowed to register.

In April 1990 mid-level officers attempted unsuccessfully to overthrow the government of Babangida in which 69 people were accused plotters and were executed after secret trials before military tribunals.

At the beginning of December 1990 the first stage of partisan elections was held at the local government level. There was low number of turnout and there was no violence in the electoral activities and the two parties competed favorably in all the regions of the country. The SDP won majority of the local government councils.

Starting from December 1991 state legislative elections were held and Babangida established a decree that allowed the previously banned politicians to join in the contest in the primaries scheduled ahead of August 1991. The elections were canceled as a result of fraud and electoral malpractices; even subsequent primaries scheduled for the month of September were also canceled. All announced candidates were disqualified from contesting for president hence a new election platform was selected.

THE JUNE 12 CHAOS

Finally in June 12, 1993 the presidential election was held and the inauguration and swearing in of the new president was scheduled to take place on 27 August 1993, the eighth anniversary of General Babangida's coming to power.

In the historic 12 June 1993 presidential elections, which most observers deemed to be Nigeria's fairest election; early returns indicated that wealthy Yoruba businessman M. K. O. Abiola won a decisive victory. However, on 23 June, Babangida, using several pending lawsuits annulled the election, throwing Nigeria into turmoil.

More than 100 people were killed in riots before Babangida reconsidered handing power to an interim government on 27 August 1993. He afterward attempted to cancel this decision, since he had less popular and military support, he was forced to hand over to Ernest Shonekan, a prominent nonpartisan businessman. Shonekan was to rule until elections scheduled for February 1994. Although he had led Babangida's Transitional Council since 1993, Shonekan was unable to reverse Nigeria's economic problems or to minimise lingering political tension and agitation.

THE SANI ABACHA NINTH MILITARY COUP

On 17 November 1993 the interim civilian government of Shonekan was overthrown by the Defense Minister General Sani Abacha. Abacha dissolved all democratic institutions and replaced elected governors with military officers.

Abacha promised to restore Nigeria to civilian rule but he did not make public the timeline of events of restoration to civilian rule. The reasons Abacha gave for overthrowing the interim civilian government of Earnest Shonekan was that there was socio-political uncertainties.

Abacha and a Regime of Power

Abacha established a decree in 1994 that made him autocratic and above the law. Although all the military regimes did; but Abacha wield one of the outstanding military influence that further corrupt the Nigerian Police Force. He reorganized the police unit to suit his concern and used it in the most authoritarian way; all in the bid to consolidate his power. In 1998 General Abacha attempted to convert himself from military head of government to civilian president. Abacha ran a military regime that was faulted in so many ways and involved in abuses of human right. Abacha died in the Presidential villa-Aso Rock on June 8, 1998.

Abacha and Economic Achievement

Nigeria was still on its colorful oil boom during Abacha's regime. Abacha raised the foreign exchange reserves[10] from

---

[10] Foreign exchange reserves are cash and other reserve assets saved with the central bank of a country or any other monetary institution authorized and competent to balance the country's

$494 million from 1993 to $9.6 billion toward the middle of 1997. He defrayed part of the external debt of Nigeria from $36 billion from 1993 to $27 billion as at 1997. He lowered the Nigerian inflation rate of 54% which was inherited from Ernest Shonekan to 8.5% from 1993 to 1998. Abacha constructed many urban roads in many Nigerian major cities from Kano to Port Harcort. Nigerian crude oil was sold at $15 per barrel.

Abacha and Nigerian Corruption Level

There was huge amount of money laundering. Billions of dollars were heard moved to overseas banks and offshore accounts. As the economy soared so the level of corruption as well soared. It was General Abacher's ingenuity that the country be re-zoned into six zones so as to popularly represent the country's multi-ethnic, economic enterprising, political realities and human resources:

---

foreign financial transactions which also influence the foreign exchange rate of the country's currency, and boost confidence in financial markets. Reserves are normally maintained in dollar or Euro.

North Central	North East	North West	South East	South South	South West
Benue State,	Adamawa State,	Jigawa State,	Abia State,	Akwa Ibom State,	Ekiti State,
Cogi State,	Bauchi State,	Kaduna State,	Anambra State,	Bayelsa State,	Lagos State,
Kwara State,	Borno State,	Kano State,	Ebonyi State,	Cross River State,	Ogun State,
Nasarawa State,	Gombe State,	Katsina State,	Enugu State,	Delta State,	Ondo State,
Niger State,	Taraba State,	Kebbi State,	Imo State	Edo State,	Osun State,
Plateau State,	Yobe State	Sokoto State,		River State,	Oyo State
Federal Cpt. Abuja		Zamfara State			

Following the annulment of the June 12 election the United States and others imposed sanctions on Nigeria including travel restrictions on government officials and suspension of arms sales and military assistance. Additional sanctions were imposed as a result of Nigeria's failure to gain full certification for its counter-narcotics efforts.

Although Abacha was initially welcomed by many Nigerians but no sooner had he overstayed his welcome than disenchantment grew rapidly. Opposition leaders formed the National Democratic Coalition (NADECO), which campaigned to reconvene the Senate and other disbanded democratic institutions.

On 11 June 1994 Moshood Kashimawo Olawale Abiola declared himself president and went into hiding until his arrest on 23 June. In response petroleum workers called a strike demanding that Abacha release Abiola and hand over power to him. Other unions joined the strike, bringing economic life around Lagos and the southwest to a standstill.

After calling off a threatened strike in July the Nigeria Labour Congress (NLC) reconsidered a general strike in August after the government imposed conditions on Abiola's release.

On 17 August 1994 the government dismissed the leadership of the NLC and the petroleum unions, placed the unions under appointed administrators, and arrested Frank Kokori and other labor leaders.

TENTH MILITARY COUP AND FORTH UNSUCCESSFUL COUP ATTEMPT

The government alleged in early 1995 that military officers and civilians were engaged in a coup plot. Security officers rounded up the accused, including former Head of State Obasanjo and his deputy, retired General Shehu Musa Yar'Adua. After a secret tribunal most of the accused were convicted and several death sentences were handed down.

In 1994 the government set up the Ogoni Civil Disturbances Special Tribunal to try Ogoni activist Ken Saro-Wiwa and others for their alleged roles in the killings of four Ogoni politicians. The tribunal sentenced Saro-Wiwa and eight others to death and they were executed on 10 November 1995.

On 1 October 1995 Abacha announced the timetable for a three-year transition to civilian rule. Only five political parties were approved by the regime and voter turnout for local elections in December 1997 was under 10%.

ELEVENTH MILITARY COUP AND FIFTH UNSUCCESSFUL MILITARY COUP ATTEMPT

On 20 December 1997 the government arrested General Oladipo Diya, ten officers, and eight civilians on charges of coup plotting. The accused were tried before a Gen Victor Malu military tribunal in which Diya and five others- Late Gen AK Adisa, Gen Tajudeen Olanrewaju, Late Col OO Akiyode, Major Seun Fadipe and a civilian Engr. Bola Adebanjo were sentenced to death to die by firing squad.

Abacha enforced authority through the federal security system which is accused of numerous human rights abuses, including infringements on freedom of speech, assembly, association, travel, and violence against women.

Abubakar's Transition to Civilian Rule

Abacha died of heart failure on 8 June 1998 and General Abdulsalami Abubakar became the head of the government known as the Military Provisional Ruling Council (PRC). The government commuted the sentences of those accused in the alleged coup during the Abacha regime and released almost all known civilian political detainees. Since the constitution written in 1995 was yet to be promulgated, the government observed some provisions of the 1979 and 1989 constitutions; since neither Abacha nor Abubakar lifted the decree suspending the 1979 constitution, and the 1989 constitution.

There was corruption in the judicial system, security sector and dearth resources. By way of solving the problems Abubakar's government implemented a civil service pay increase and other reforms.

In August 1998 Abubakar appointed the Independent National Electoral Commission (INEC) to conduct elections for local government councils, state legislatures and governors, the national assembly, and president. The NEC successfully held elections on 5 December 1998, 9 January 1999, 20 February, and 27 February 1999, respectively. For local elections nine parties were granted provisional registration with three fulfilling the requirements to contest the following elections.

These parties were the People's Democratic Party (PDP), the All People's Party (APP), and the predominantly Yoruba Alliance for Democracy (AD). Former military head of state Olusegun Obasanjo, freed from prison by Abubakar, ran as a civilian candidate and won the presidential election.

The PRC promulgated a new constitution based largely on the suspended 1979 constitution, before the 29 May 1999 inauguration of the new civilian president. The constitution includes provisions for a bicameral legislature, the National Assembly consisting of a 360-member House of Representatives and a 109-member Senate.

THE FOURTH REPUBLIC

The month of May 1999 marked the end of 16 straight years of military rule in Nigeria and the emergence of democratically elected government. Thanks to General Olusegun Obasanjo in 1979 and thanks to General Abdulsalami Abubakar in 1999. The emergence of democracy in Nigeria on May 1999 ended 16 years of consecutive military rule. Olusegun Obasanjo was the first military head of state who handed power over to civilian in 1979. It was he, as a civilian to whom the presidency was handed over by another military head of state after twenty years; can you imagine the mystery of the passage of time and happenstance…

Olusegun Obasanjo handed over power to civilian president in 1979, a country booming with affluence but he inherited a country whose economy is not only stagnant but backward and the deterioration of most democratic institutions and systems in 1999.

Obasanjo is a former army general with clean records. He stood taller than any military head or dictators in Nigeria. He is admired for his courage and record of returning the Nigerian government to civilian rule in 1979 and for receiving it back in 1999.

He took over a country that faced many problems, including a dysfunctional bureaucracy, collapsed infrastructure, and a military with undying urge for corruption and power that wanted a reward for returning to settle quietly for good at the barracks.

The President quickly retired hundreds of military officers holding political positions and established a panel to investigate human rights violations, released hundreds of persons held without charge, and canceled many questionable licenses and contracts left by the previous regimes. The government also tried to recover billions of Naira and dollars spirited away to overseas and offshore accounts.

With the Nigerian representational and young democracy, conflicts still persist between the Executive and Legislative branches over appropriations, funds and other proposed legislation. This is a sign that true and thorough federalism is needed in the growing visibility and diversity of states, administrative tools and dynamics and the inherent friction between Abuja and the state capitals over resource allocation.

What is the best solution to the situation? Every right thinking person has seen that bureaucracy of Abuja resources and allocation, the scrambling for state allocation and the waste and delay of time are not included as part of leadership flaws. These are challenges for every thinking person to look towards another direction of solution to the Nigeria problems.

Sectarian and domestic violence, growing agitation for resources sharing has plagued the Obasanjo government since its inception. In May 1999 violence erupted in Kaduna State over the succession of an Emir resulting in more than 100 deaths. In November 1999, the army destroyed the town of Odi, Bayelsa State and killed scores of civilians in retaliation for the murder of 12 policemen by a local gang. In Kaduna in February through May 2000 over 1,000 people died in rioting over the introduction of criminal Shar'ia in the State. Hundreds of ethnic Hausa were killed in reprisal attacks in south-eastern Nigeria. In September 2001, over 2,000 people were killed in inter-religious rioting in Jos. In October 2001, hundreds were killed and thousands displaced in communal violence that spread across the states of Benue, Taraba, and Nasarawa. On 1 October 2001 Obasanjo announced the formation of a National Security Commission to address the issue of violence.

Obasanjo was reelected in 2003. The new president faces the daunting task of rebuilding a petroleum-based economy, whose revenues have been squandered through corruption and mismanagement. Additionally, the Obasanjo administration must move to defuse longstanding ethnic and religious tensions if it hopes to build a foundation for economic growth and political stability. Currently there is conflict in the Niger Delta over the environmental destruction caused by oil drilling and the ongoing poverty in the oil-rich region.

Obasanjo's outstanding achievements include; he raised Nigerian foreign reserve from $2 billion to $43 billion from 1999 to 2007. He raised Nigerian national and international communication system by bringing the mobile telecommunications (GSM) and launched the first Nigerian satellite in space for internet access and mobile communication.

YAR' ADUA'S SICKNESS AND JONATHAN'S SUCCESSION

In the 2007 general election, Umaru Yar'Adua and Goodluck Jonathan, both of the People's Democratic Party, were elected President and Vice President, respectively. In November 2009 President Yar'Adua fell sick and was flown to Saudi Arabia for medical attention. There was no communication concerning his state of health for 50 days. As a result rumors started spreading that he had died. This continued until the BBC aired an interview that was allegedly done via telephone from the president's sick bed in Saudi Arabia. As of January 2010, he was still abroad.

In February 2010, Goodluck Jonathan began serving as acting President in the absence of Yar'Adua. In May 2010, the Nigerian government learned of Yar'Adua's death after a long battle with existing health problems and an undisclosed illness. Goodluck Jonahan the Vice President was able to manage the affairs of the country amidst the challenges from the President's ill health and death.

Goodluck Jonathan called for new elections and stood for re-election in April 2011, which he won. In 2015 he lost his re-election bid with the emergence of former military ruler General Muhammadu Buhari, mainly on his inability to quell the rising insecurity in the country. One of the outstanding achievements of Goodluck Jonathan administration was resuscitation of the railways in the country after about 30-years of non-function. Nigeria had the highest GDP and the largest economy in Africa.

Goodluck Jonathan administration built nine federal universities.

Muhammadu Buhari was declared winner of the 2015 presidential elections. Rtd. General Muhammadu Buhari took over the helm of affairs in May 2015 after a peaceful transfer of power from the Jonathan led administration.

MUHAMMADU BUHARI PRESIDENCY

There have been series of agitation on Muhammadu Buhari presidency quite the nature of Nigerian electoral campaign and election itself since the history of self-rule in Nigeria. The test of the ability to rule lies in the ruler's adaptive behavior. Sadly that Nigeria has not had the kind of leadership model governed by adaptive model of behavior. Another perspective to view those on the seat of power is through their vision of the future. The vision of the one on the seat of power has to be clarified and transparent. The vision and the common value need to be well clarified as the best part of the manifesto of the ruler or any aspirant to the seat of power. Nigeria has never had a visionary leader so far, but Nigeria has had about two or three persons in the list who have tried to show some signs that apparently they have a model of leadership that could place Nigerian future on the fast lane. Rtd. General Obasanjo had many steps ahead of every Nigerian leader. Rtd. General Abdulsalami Abubakar can be seen equally as one who demonstrated another true enthusiasm in the vocation of leadership; he overcame the temptation of lingering in power. Goodluck Jonathan manifested vision for the future of Nigerian economy. Muhammadu Buhari in his first presidency as a soldier showed zeal to restore Nigeria to moral, ethical and public dignity through autocratic force; it also reflects in his second presidency as a civilian, although with every honest intention if only he can step up his leadership with the great opportunity on his hand, many things will change and Nigerians will sing a new song with his name. Buhari is on the line to offer Nigerians the best he can if only he can pull-off completely his military autocratic uniform. He has one of the best policies to transform the Nigerian political climate.

Mr Buhari was a former army Major General who toppled the elected government of Mr. Shehu Shagari in a military coup on 31st December 1983.

Mr Buhari, the then Major General Buhari used to be the GOC-General Officer in Command of the Third Armoured Division in Jos. He appointed Tunde Idiagbon as his second in command and as his Chief of General Staff as soon as the coup was successful.

The military regime of 1983 crashed the second republic or the second democratically elected government which was brought into scene by multi-party system which begun in 1979.

Their reason for toppling the democratically elected government of Mr Shagari was that it was a government of corruption and rip-off Nigerian economy. And that such government is worse than nothing at all, this was according to the New York Times. And that the new regime was set to restore the economy and national discipline. The regime consequently suspended the constitution. All the unsuccessful and successful military coup and regime had the same basis of accusation especially for corruption as the reason for overthrowing the government but none came close to the preferred solution except for Obasanjo both as military and as civilian and Buhari.

General Buhari left a strong foot print within the short time of his military regime, although with autocratic and capital punishment measure. The war against indiscipline (WAI) inaugurated on March 20 1984 was a positive agenda with good impact nationwide. It was a policy that intended to check moral decadents of citizens' public life and civil responsibility. His autocratic traits and reliance on capital punishment earned him global criticisms.

Mr Buhari acknowledged the words of his critics and prior to the 2015 presidential election pledged that if he was elected that he would be a bearer of fair judgment, the rule of law and human rights. There are many more good qualities in Buhari. He was once the Chairman of the Petroleum Trust Fund (PTF) who managed the revenue accrued from petroleum during the regime of General Sani Abacha. Buhari earned himself and the entire country good name from the transparent way he managed the fund and responsibility entrusted on him such that the New African applauded him for a good job.

Security system is one of the defining means of stability of a country. This factor has remained a bone of contention in the history of Nigerian self-rule and one of the chief causes of indiscipline. Every past Nigerian ruler failed the test on innovativeness and ingenuity that can sustain and raise the security system of Nigeria. A socio-political group called the Northern Elders Forum even mentioned in February 2020 that the Buhari administration has also failed in the areas of security.

CHAPTER 3

THE SLAPDASH OF CAPITALIST AND SOCIALIST ECONOMIC STYLE

The slapdash economic plans results because of the centripetal economic policies that aims at "fixing"; there is synthetic attempts to determine market forces and behavior of the people; there is exploitation; until the two hinges of capitalist and communalist economy are reframed to fit the principles which dictates for federalist states the economy would remain backward in the global competition.

Not only from the perspective of political concernment, administrative enhancement, infrastructural development; the 1967 and after the war in 1970 Nigerian government took a central governance following the oil revenue explosion; hitherto the under mentioned perspectives were still to be accounted. The revenue from the oil boom was used to increase their personal income and increased job opportunities which the governing team distributed to their business partners.

With the collapse of the Nigerian economy in late 1970s and mid 1980s the ethnic regions began to grown in discontentment at the central government who started to inject hate and discontentment into the citizens against their foreign neighbors who migrated to Nigeria for greener pastures; Cameroon, Chad, Niger, Ghana etc. When these foreign neighbors were driven away from Nigeria as though it would solve the problem; Nigeria began to notice a growing discontentment not only against the government but against fellow Nigerians in an ethnic hate such that even in Lagos the Igbo people were asked to leave. The government initiated a low profile spending as mandated by the International Monetary Fund (IMF) and the World Bank. It started with the Shehu Shagari Second Republic as "Austerity Measure" across the Babangida Military Regime as "Structural Adjustment

Program". The IMF and World Bank project for reactivating the economy was on privatization exercise, price control of goods and reduction in government spending and budget. The idea was professionally derived from the principle that may be interpreted using common or lay expression thus; the masses led by the government over a period of time have reached its sort of peak spending and consumption habit such that the general productivity ability becomes low relative to what each person consume; now there must be a way to lessen peoples' habit on social and luxury goods and prioritize the essential goods. The essential goods were classified as food, clothing and shelter. This is in the face of GDP per capita fall. Essential or basic life needs should really be defined as follows:

- Fairly comfortable shelter
- Good food
- Healthcare
- Clean water

- Electricity

Nigerians deserve these even if it is in the most basic form. This is the modern basic and essential standard of living.

The Interference of SAP to Labor Market

According to the National Office of Statistics in 1985 the national unemployment rate was estimated at 4.3 percent. It increased to 5.3 percent during 1986. It increased again to 7.0 in 1987. Because of the measures introduced under SAP the unemployment rate falls to 5.1 percent in 1988.

Agricultural Activities

In 1959 the Nigerian GDP from the agricultural sector was 65.7 percent and after seventeen years, in 1976 the GDP shrank to 30.9, with 34.8 percent decrease. After twelve years, in 1988 the GDP was 39.1 percent; an increase of 8.2 percent was recorded.

The overall GDP from agricultural sector from 1959 to 1988 recorded a decreased agricultural activity of 26.6 percent. Notices of increase happened between 1983-1988; the agricultural sector contributed to the Nigerian economy with an increase of 3.8 percent every year from 1983-1988. The percentile from the export value from agriculture increased from 3 percent in 1983 to 9 percent in 1988. These increase happened mostly because of the fall in oil export income. Again after the exchange-rate reform placed restriction on food importation in 1986 there was increase in local food production.

The Manufacturing Sector

Although the agricultural sector's contribution to the Country's GDP was going down, the manufacturing share of the GDP was going up with the record of 4.4 percent in 1959 to 9.4 percent in 1970. In 1973 during the oil boom it falls to 7.0 percent. It subsequently increased to 11.4 percent in 1981 and declined again to 10.0 percent in 1988. The overall statistics of manufacturing activities from 1959-1988 showed a decline of -1.6 percent share of the GDP. This can further be interpreted like a drama of child's learning to walk; the child was only able to do 3 steps forward and 5 steps backward. During the 1970s for the manufacturing sectors, the use of tariff manipulations helped mere assembly business and activities of imported products and helped only in a little way concerning the indigenous effort to add value to imported manufactured products. It no doubt helped in little ways concerning employment. The major disadvantage was that manufacturing and industrial growth was very slow. Goods such as vegetable oil, milled grain refined sugar, soft drinks, can foods, textile material, jewelry, wood, footwear, tires, tubes, glass, cement, metal objects, bricks, electrical parts for household use, radios, motor parts were all produced in Nigerian or assembled. The value added in manufacturing shrank by 25 percent between 1982-1986 because of incompetence in allocation of resources and price falsification and also as a result of tariff in import or restriction of importation including exports and import substitutes.

Structural Adjustment Program (SAP) contributed positively towards the increase in manufacturing sector's contribution to GDP in 1986 through 1988 up to 8 percent. The privatization exercise was the brain behind this.

The Indigenization Policy

From foreign majority ownership to indigenous majority ownership of shares in many industries the Nigerian Enterprises Promotion Decree of 1972, 1977 and 1981 was implemented to limit foreign ownership of shares in industries. From 1960s to late 1970s there was a system of industrial activities in the manufacturing sector that permitted foreign ownership or foreign majority ownership of shares which Nigeria benefited. The Nigerian Business moguls influenced the government to implement policies that encouraged indigenization of industries. (If the government had remained with full federalism as a principle and practice it would not have been so that the business people would influence the government to take a course of action that was premature in the industrial and manufacturing sector). Foreigners in that process were mandated to sell their ownership and shares to the rich Nigerians mainly, military leaders, top civil servants and other professionals became rich overnight. Towards the middle of 1988 the government already saw the mistakes on premature indigenization decree and policy and began to relax the indigenization decree. Foreign investors were given the opportunity to hold shares again in various sectors.

Energy, Mining and Oil

Tin and columbite production reduced from 1960s to 1980s. In 1980s a small quantity of deposit of iron ore was mined. Uranium was also found. There is considerable dependence on hydroelectricity in Nigeria. Coal mining and coal production shrank from 1958-1986, from 940,000 tons to 73,000 respectively. The use of coal as energy has become so minimal that only 1 percent of the commercial activities apply coal. Two-thirds of the energy in Nigeria is acquired from petroleum since the 1990s and has remained the indomitable Nigerian mineral exports. Mining contributed 1.0 percent of GDP in 1959 and together with petroleum they made up to 14 percent in 1988.

Finance and Banking

The Nigeria's first bank, the African Banking Corporation was established in 1892 and it existed for sixty years before banking legislation began in Nigeria in 1952. The 1952 banking ordinance set the rules and standard for reserve funds and institute banking examinations and established assistance for indigenous banking system. The time was set for real banking business and Nigeria had the first three foreign banks; the Bank of British West Africa, the Barclays Bank, and the British and French Bank, followed by two indigenous banks; the National Bank of Nigeria and the African Continental Bank. However, it is interesting to note that for over twenty years Nigerians remained reluctant to accept checks for settlement of debts; they preferred cash. This fact slowed down the growth of demand deposits and withdrawal for decades. The West African Currency Board was established by the British in 1912 to enable the financial transactions of export trade of foreign companies operating in West Africa in order to issue a West African currency convertible to British pounds. At that time British policies disallowed local investment of reserves, deposit expansion, discretion to manage money and training Africans to develop indigenous financial institutions. Some Nigerian members of the federal House of Assembly in 1952 raised the opinion for the establishment of a central bank to facilitate economic development. The motion was defeated and British administration appointed a Bank of England official to study the situation. The outcome of the study was that the Nigerian capital market and the environment were still undeveloped and that the issue of establishing a central bank was impracticable. After five years, in 1957 the colonial administration conducted another study which approved of the establishment of a Nigerian central bank together and introduced a Nigerian currency. (It is worthy of note that for all the steps that the colonial administration was to take they involved a series of serious, honest and diligent study of the issue and the situation).

The Nigerian pound was on the same exchange rate with the British pound until the British currency's devaluation in 1967 and the Nigerian currency was converted in 1973 to a decimal currency, the naira (N), equivalent to two old Nigerian pounds.

The smallest unit of the new currency was the kobo, 100 of which equaled 1 naira.

The naira, which exchanged for US$1.52 in January 1973 and again in March 1982 (or N0.67 = US$1), despite the floating exchange rate, depreciated relative to the United States dollar in the 1980s.

The average exchange rate in 1990 was N8.004 = US$1. Depreciation accelerated after the creation of a second-tier foreign exchange market under World Bank structural adjustment in September 1986.

The Central Bank of Nigeria, which was statutorily independent of the federal government until 1968, began operations on July 1, 1959. Following a decade of struggle over the relationship between the government and the Central Bank, a 1968 military decree granted authority over banking and monetary policy to the Federal Executive Council.

The role of the Central Bank, similar to that of central banks in North America and Western Europe, was to establish the Nigerian currency, control and regulate the banking system, serve as banker to other banks in Nigeria, and carry out the government's economic policy in the monetary field.

The policy included control of bank credit growth, credit distribution by sector, cash reserve requirements for commercial banks, discount - rates-interest rates the Central Bank charged commercial and merchant banks and the ratio of banks' long-term assets to deposits. Changes in Central Bank restrictions on credit and monetary expansion affected total demand and income. For example, in 1988, as inflation accelerated, the Central Bank tried to restrain monetary growth.

The Nigerian government suspended dividend repatriation and profits to the parents companies overseas during the civil war. (Was that the due process of punishment to the mother companies overseas?) Foreign travel allowances were reduced including allowances to be paid for overseas public offices and demanded permission before any foreign payment must be made. The Nigerian government went on and issued new currency notes to replace the existing ones in January 1968. In 1970 the Central Bank advised the government not to be too fast to dismantle import and financial constraints after the war. (But since it is a case of a Judge giving judgment in his own case; what would you expect?). Soon in 1970 the oil boom set in and the complacency of lifestyle of the government officials and freedom from restrictions prevailed.

The three largest commercial banks held about one-third of total bank deposits. In 1973 the federal government undertook to acquire a 40-percent equity ownership of the three largest foreign banks. In 1976, under the second Nigerian Enterprises Promotion Decree requiring 60-percent indigenous holdings, the federal government acquired an additional 20-percent holding in the three largest foreign banks and 60-percent ownership in the other foreign banks. Yet indigenization did not change the management, control, and lending orientation toward international trade, particularly of foreign companies and their Nigerian subsidiaries of foreign banks.

At the end of 1988, the banking system consisted of the Central Bank of Nigeria, forty-two commercial banks, and twenty four merchant banks, a substantial increase since 1986. Merchant banks were allowed to open checking accounts for corporations only and could not accept deposits below N50,000. Commercial and merchant banks together had 1,500 branches in 1988, up from 1,000 in 1984. In 1988 commercial banks had assets of N52.2 billion compared to N12.6 billion for merchant banks in early 1988. In 1990 the government put N503 million into establishing community banks to encourage community development associations, cooperative societies, farmers' groups, patriotic unions, trade groups, and other local organizations, especially in rural areas.

Other financial institutions included government-owned specialized development banks: the Nigerian Industrial Development Bank, the Nigerian Bank for Commerce and Industry, and the Nigerian Agricultural Bank, as well as the

Federal Savings Banks and the Federal Mortgage Bank. Also active in Nigeria were numerous insurance companies, pension funds, and finance and leasing companies. Nigeria also had a stock exchange (established in Lagos in 1961) and a number of stockbrokerage firms. The Securities and Exchange Commission (SEC) Decree of 1988 gave the Nigerian SEC powers to regulate and supervise the capital market. These powers included the right to revoke stockbroker registrations and approve or disapprove any new stock exchange. Established in 1988, the Nigerian Deposit Insurance Corporation increased confidence in the banks by protecting depositors against bank failures in licensed banks up to N50,000 in return for an annual bank premium of nearly 1 percent of total deposit liabilities.

Finance and insurance services represented more than 3 percent of Nigeria's GDP in 1988. Economists agree that services, consisting disproportionately of nonessential items, tend to expand as a share of national income as national economy grows (is that not a sign of complacency and luxurious living?). However, Nigeria, lacked comparable statistics over an extended period, preventing generalizations about the service sector. Statistics indicate, nevertheless, that services went from 28.9 percent of GDP in 1981 to 31.1 percent in 1988, a period of no economic growth (A Period of no economic growth?). In 1988 services comprised the following percentages of GDP: wholesale and retail trade, 17.1 percent; hotels and restaurants, less than 1 percent; housing, 2.0 percent; government services, 6. percent; real estate and business services, less than 1 percent; and other services, less than 1 percent. (Cf. Facts about Nigeria http://worldfacts.us/Nigeria.htm)

Objective Planning (Strategy)

It was learned that the British administration had no proper and comprehensive plan on how to run the affairs of Nigeria before 1945. (Cf. the Suggestions of the British Nobel Economist Sir William Arthur Lewis and Sayre P. Schatz on the weaknesses of Nigeria after the Civil War). The known national development plan for Nigeria began 1946 to 1962; these were all British framed plans for Nigerian national development and for Nigerian economy.

Could it be true that Nigerian leadership had no objective strategic plan for National development right from the end of the Civil War? Maybe because the leadership is motivated by the winner takes it all; because the so-called winners of the war have been the same group who has led the country for three score years. Most of the projects made for development affected the material welfare of the people, Central Bank policies, regional state's development, Ministry of Education, and Marketing Boards etc. "The main weaknesses of Nigerian development were incomplete feasibility studies and inadequate evaluation of projects, accompanied by meager public participation, followed by excessive political intervention in economic decisions and centralized decision pattern. Moreover, insufficient attention was paid to the small indigenous sector, and the machinery for implementing developments in the public sector was unsatisfactory". These were the hindsight of the foreign economists and authors. And these authors favored decentralized decision making.[11]

THE SOCIAL MARKET ECONOMY

The idea of social market economy, or Rhine capitalism or social capitalism, is a political ideology and a socioeconomic model which juggles together a free market capitalist economy with social policies that establish both fair competition within the market and a welfare state.

At times the social market economy is taken to mean a coordinated market economy in which commerce and industry are owned and run by individuals in order to make for equity and opportunity for a smoother level-playing ground of social and

---

[11] Ibid, Suggestions of the British Nobel Economist Sir William Arthur Lewis and Sayre P. Schatz on the weaknesses of Nigeria after the Civil War

environmental responsibility. The social market economy has given people greater opportunity to take responsibility not in a small measure but in the most accountable and transparent ways. All business conferences emphasize this element of social market economy either with words or through diagram. The truth is that Nigerian business benchmark has not placed this element of social and business responsibility on priority.

Rhine capitalism or social capitalism, Tristan Claridge (2017) is a socioeconomic model combining a free market capitalist economic system alongside social policies that establish both fair competition within the market and a welfare state. ("Social Market". Economics Dictionary. *The Economist*).

It is sometimes classified as a coordinated market economy. Kopst in & Lichbach 2005) The social market economy was originally promoted and implemented in West Germany by the Christian Democratic Union (CDU) under Chancellor Konrad Adenauer in 1949. Spicka (2007) its origins can be traced to the inter war Freiburg school of economic thought. Steffen Mau (2003).

The social market economy was designed to be a third way between *laissez-faire* economic liberalism and socialist economics. Abelshauser (2004).

It was strongly inspired by Ordo Liberalism, Nils Goldschmidt, Hermann Rauchenschwandtner (2007). Social democratic reformism and the political ideology of Christian democracy or more generally the tradition of Christian ethics. Lamberts, Emiel (1997).

The Nigerian social market economy should refrain from attempts to plan, guide and fix production, the workforce, or sales; nevertheless, it should be anything but not chaos. It should support planned efforts to positively influence the economy through the organic means of a comprehensive economic policy forged with flexible adaptation to market behavior and studies. By combining monetary, credit, trade, tax, customs, investment and social policies as well as other measures, this type of economic policy must aim to create an economy for Nigerians to serves the welfare and needs of the entire population, enhance infrastructural development and create more jobs and by so doing fulfill the ultimate goal of providing opportunity for young and growing investors and quell the survival of the fittest spirit and also aim at flattening the curve between the rich and the poor.

THE NIGERIAN ECONOMIC PATTERN

The economy of Nigeria has two Phases: the capitalist and the communist. This is because there are some areas of the pattern where it is allowed for free market and competition and there are some areas that are not free for all, the government itself owns or controls those areas. This is an interaction between capitalism and communalism and such economic system is plausible to ensure growth, hard-work, and stability and to control undue forces and frustration to free market initiative; it is a kind of mixed economy. However, it is still difficult to evaluate the success of such an economic style based on which of these systems has protected the wealth of the country more from selfish-interest or how both has helped towards yielding economic advancement on the country.

The leadership and the government may have to review the corporate and business environment to enable:

- The private sector
- Price control system
- Minimize levies and taxes
- Organized labor market
- Encourage vocational training (Adult Schooling)
- Organized transport system
- Electricity infrastructure to stabilize power

Through these means the country's lifestyle, standard of living, identity and self image and satisfaction may be redeemed.

What is irksome about the Nigerian double phases of economic model is that even though the model is one of the most progressive approached by many developed economies of the world; the irony is that it does not work or the yield is very meager and the economy is very slow. It is very absurd that some of the features and trade-offs making up the capitalist model are weak; for instance:

- The process of acquisition of private property (business confidence)
- Self-interest benefit
- Freedom of choice (free market)
- Competition

With the vulnerability of policy of trade protectionism; business confidence is gone, self-interest action is weakened, and freedom of choice is lost, competition becomes a stage managed dominion and the economy stifles. What is the use of all the Nigerian business conferences?

What the socio-economic climate of the government has as trade-offs and as key factors of socialist economy are equally weak; for instance:

- Imbalance distribution of some power and control to business owners

- Imbalance distribution of consumption

- Limited protection to up-coming businesses in certain markets

- Un-even tax incentive provision for monopolistic industries

There are reasons to support the argument that the shallow federalist system of Nigerian government gives rise to the only socialist element in the government in terms that the government solely takes decisions pertaining to economic strategy. Such haphazard federalist model gives rise to weak security system and weak supervision. Is this not a structured failure from the constitution to the economic policies and leadership? Some of the functions of good leadership include:

- Direction – the leader communicates the goal of the government both short term and long term and the process towards achieving the goals.
- The leader provides the atmosphere proper to achieve economic stability through transparency and implementation of transparent policies.
- The leader has the function to bridge personal interest with that of organizational/institutional and economic interest in order to avoid conflict.
- Intelligence – effective leadership counts on the mature behavior, balance personality, quick problem tackling mind of the leader etc.
- Effective leadership is able to interpret the dynamics in productive ability in an industrial economy and derive

the best of approach from the best possible result by ensuring best positive influence.

SOCIAL ECONOMICS, SOCIAL CAPITAL, SOCIAL MARKET IN NIGERIA

Social economics is an academic discipline; a social science which analyzes a country's economic activities as they are shaped by the social life of the people in particular and in general it discusses on the influence of the modern nations' economies vis a vis social affairs and the progression or retrogression or their stagnation. Since societal affairs are split in three phases: social, economic and cultural. So social economics can also apply to how social and economic factors affect the environment and lifestyle of the people.

- So how has Nigerian social and economic affairs affected the entire Nigerian environment and the lifestyle of Nigerians? This question would lead to a critical reflection of the chronology of Nigerian history,

Nigerian leadership approach, and the haphazard federalist style of Nigerian government, the slapdash of capitalist and socialist economic style and the perennial agitation of Nigerians. This is what this book is all about.

The Pursuit of Self-Interest in the Disproportionate Gap between the Rich and the Poor

On another perspective, contemporary thoughts reflect on human behavior and interactions of individuals and groups in the light of the concept: social "capital" and social "markets".

Social capital is the effective functioning of social groups through interpersonal relationships, a shared sense of identity, a shared understanding, shared norms, shared values, trust, cooperation, and reciprocity. Will Kenton (2019). This setting is still lacking in the Nigerian sociopolitical, economical and cultural. The will to cheat and to defraud translates in the lifestyle of "survival of the fittest" is an alarming element of individual and group life in such a way as though nobody cares.

Social capital is the product of good human interaction favorable and positive. It may be concrete, tangible or intangible. It includes:

- Ideas that are innovative for business
- Opportunities for growth in business
- Shared ideas and values
- Common purpose
- Sense of belonging
- Mutual respect and trust
- Information that are useful in business or for life
- It excludes the will to cheat and to defraud.

The Nigerian education system may consider restructuring its curriculum as a way of re-emphasizing and re-energizing the spirit and sense of social competence and social capital.

The concept of social capital when specifically directed to business means contributing to the communal progress and success of an organization, group or country in terms of building respect and personal and corporate networks or relationship and trust for the group-work cohesion to enhance performance and productivity.

The social media and internet has favored the school in our room and has transformed social capital in such a way as to connect with infinite number of people and sell a product with a click. Thanks to the leadership that brought Nigeria up to the use of the cellular phone and the internet about twenty years ago. Within an approximation of twenty years in the presence of the technology of cellular phone and the internet Nigerian lifestyle and Nigerian environment is changing dramatically.

The Rich getting Richer and the Poor Getting Poorer Syndrome with reference to Economic Centered/Advantaged Areas

There is a socioeconomic disease in the concept that the rich is getting richer and the poor is getting poorer. This is true for individuals and more for environments in Nigerian setting for over three score years. A person's human capital is the aggregation of knowledge and experience, good habits and social status, skill and personality, creative ability and economic prospect but this is less true in Nigeria; a person's human capital is the ability to defraud and remain shrewd.

This is the situation because humans seek survival as their first and basic instinct. Everybody seeks survival and it is a matter of how one makes the best use of one's natural gifts, beginning with the early environments. We learned from economic concept that where the proclivity for economic prosperity is; more people tend to settle there for both natural and security, commercial and economic reasons. Out of this economic struggle certain dilemma ensue which brought about the influx of people and industry in one or few places and leaving other places empty. This practice has weakened the Nigerian economy for too long. On the same note; because many people have little or no choice therefore, brain drain results as a problem in which human capital are drawn from different parts of the globe in favor of one region. Such situation is not without attendant problems: industrial productivity soon would fall below productive expectation and continue to diminish and retrogress. In that case, what remains is the past glory and prestige rather than further development; that brings the presence of the rich getting richer and the poor getting poorer. When economy is diversified, wealth and means are as well diversified; but when some areas are starved of the wealth and means, it creates the opportunity of the rich getting richer and the poor getting poorer. Such syndrome brings about overpopulation and complacency and diminishing value of human resources as unemployment sets in at the long run; loss of direction and motivation, over dependence on pedigree and past prestige and status quo etc. The same is true with the

Nigerian sub-national brain drain happening in Lagos and Abuja. All roads lead to Lagos or Abuja is a mentality and a disease that has killed Nigerian developmental structure.

Mottled Development

There is an irregular pattern of development in Nigeria. Such inconsistent development was set in by the central system whereby the state governors were treated with somewhat preferential gestures for those who were in good friendly order with the central power. And some governors who were unbridled hide under such central lopsidedness and loopholes and loiter with the quota they have received no matter how big or little.

Such lopsided development has spawned complexity of problems which was responsible for Nigerian massive nationwide poverty, insurgencies – agitations and rebellions for inequalities in the country spanning six decades from independence. If you blame the state governors they will in turn blame the federal government. If you blame the federal government, the federal government will blame the state government. Is that not a constitutional conspiracy? Is that not a systemic conspiracy?

SYSTEMIC EXPLOITATION

In the federal governance setting, exploitation may be minimized because each state is likely to look within its resources and negotiate for the resources that are without. Each state may be able to develop the talents of their citizens and market them with greater personal involvement.

Each state may be able to nourish their citizens with sense of belonging and commitment so as to benefit from their citizens unalloyed participation in building the state.

Accountability and transparency is a historical element of leadership which may once more become the highest value shared among the leader and the subject as the leader becomes more a model and pattern of the smaller whole and face the subjects on one to one bases making it possible that everyone feels the rewarding impacts of states' dreams and aspirations where leadership decisions involve the commitment of the leader and the followers. In that case, the state makes greater positive contribution to the people through the ability of governing group to inspire the followers. This is also the expectation and responsibility of the federal center. This would reduce the hurricane desire for power whether at the central level or at the state level because the challenge of leadership in effect draws attention on the skill and responsibility, rather than desiring for power for its own sake.

Subsidiary power and responsibility would offer greater opportunity for each state to understand what the goals of the state government and whose blame it is if such goals amount to a setback to the state. It would shed light on the responsibility, transparency, accountability and innovativeness of the leader; above all the leader is not just on the spot light of the federal center but on the constant reach out with the followers.

It would make the state more the home of every citizen of the state and afford them the right, dignity, home advantage and fear of doing something that may tarnish the public image of the state.

That would mean a modification of the definition of the state to include not just a place where a person was born but a place where a person lives and contributes from ones resources to develop. It would quell the unwarranted prejudices of "he is from the north, he is from the south, or he is from the east". Hence citizens of every state by virtue of such principle are defined by the common commitment, interest and residence, rather than by ethnic or religious prejudices.

Exploitation is violation of rights and opportunities of realizing peoples' greater potentials. Exploitation is acting unfairly against or in control of the will of a person or group of persons advertently or inadvertently.

The unitary pattern of governance is rarely free of exploitative aim especially for states that have multi-ethnic environment. Nigerians young and old, especially young skilled Nigerians have been long exploited by the unitary system of governance intentionally and unintentionally. One who understands the past history of Nigeria would recollect the incident before the Nigerian civil war of the riots started by the Institute of Management and the students of Ahmadu Belo University Jos. The students started the riot in order to resist the emerging constitution that reintroduced the unitary system for fear that it would deny the region the opportunity to develop itself with the resources taped from the region. The students had to rampage against the regime of General Johnson Aguiyi Ironsi.

As defined by social theories all systems of modern government may pretend to ensure the wellbeing of its citizens, yet they keep hidden intent because they remain merely agents of exploitation especially when they are manned by morally impugned ruler. The unitary governance provides such tainted pattern for a very big nation like Nigeria the giant of Africa; which is why her development remains tainted.

Social psychology defines distributive justice as a perceived fairness of how rewards and costs are shared (distributed across) by group members. For example, when workers of the same job and same qualification are paid different salaries, group members are likely to feel that the principle of distributive justice has not been justified. This is an exploitative intent packaged in the unitary system of governance, especially to mock skilled individuals, semiskilled workers and professionals; and to siphon their skill and to discourage every inspiration or aspiring spirit and bore up-coming individuals. That is a very big disease that has weakened the Nigerian talents from the root of education up to the practice of skills.

Individuals in a state have a way to know whether the principle of distributive justice has been satisfied by observing the distributive norms of their counterparts, or by comparing their own work satisfaction and comfort across their neighboring groups. This is an indispensable constituent of the competitive level-ground which is the catalyst for talents and strong economy.

The state which remains outstanding in rewards and cost distribution and in maintaining the standard of living and designed distributive norms surely is the state that would be seen as the pace setter or trailblazer for others. This is a viable economic situation where citizens measure their success by the success of the state; if the state is successful the individual talent and worker in the state would be as well successful; this is a vice versa and win-win situation.

Deprivation/Marginalization and Migration

Deprivation is torture. By depriving people access to the merited social rights you torture them psychologically. The condition produces a prolonged effect which will reflect on moral decadents and physical deterioration of health and the worst effect would be represented in the inability of the people to access critical thought thereby they lost the ability to choose; in such situation people may be forced to throw caution to the wind and take risks that may be judged irrational; for instance people taking all sorts of risks just to get outside the shores of the country.

Marginalization has remained a sore topic in the stories and complaint of almost all the thirty six states in Nigeria. Every state complains of being marginalized and denied of various deserved value.

Mankind has history of looking beyond one's immediate environment to satisfy a need. Cross-border search for need satisfaction is a right bestowed by international law. This means that certain prerequisite conditions are to be complied for cross-border search for better life. It is worthy of saying that some of the prerequisites are already provided or were to be provided by the government of origin of the citizen; for instance proper documentary evidence of the citizen's background, good education to citizens to afford a skill for survival, sense of home-advantage, easy access to the negotiating table for international transaction – the secured legal travelling papers, etc. These are the concerns of a government that is responsible for the welfare of its citizens. In those countries where these prerequisites exist only three out of ten may be willing to seek greener pasture across and beyond their own confines.

Migration desire today among Nigerians is quite baffling. One begs the question of why people itch to migrate to another country even though there may not be assured easy means of survival. Nigeria is becoming one of the top countries whose citizens are willing to defile immigration rules with careless and carefree in order to go abroad. The inferred instinct behind such behavior is that "since we are not cared for by our government why will we care for what honors our life or our government"? This is why respect and dignity and caution are thrown to the wind against patriotism. Could you believe that some Nigerians developed phobia of introducing themselves as Nigerians abroad? May be because of the horrible situation they have gone through? To do what honors one's country is patriotism and it is a sign that one loves one's country. To itch to go abroad because one is not comfortable with one's country is either motivated by the instability of the means of survival or because of deprivation or marginalization. All these are discrediting on both the government and the citizens.

The total federalization of the country would speed up development and discourage the causes of citizens itching to migrate to another country. In totally federalizing the country more skilled laborers and workers and professionals would be saved the risk of running after greener pastures across the border; especially the centuries-old insurrections and agitations and rebellions would be quelled.

Unitary governance is very outmoded and obsolete to such a vast ethnic group and multi-culture and skillful Nigerians; it sets in suffering, lack of opportunity, deprivation and marginalization which bring about laziness, corruption and illegal and involuntary migration. It can mean lack of life's necessities; it can be privation of social importance and worth; it can be reduction of normal social and cultural interaction and more. These can sometimes be the cause or consequence of drug addiction, mental illness, poverty state of living, poor education, low socioeconomic status and low sense of oneself etc.

The socially deprived person may as well experience deprivation of basic capabilities and potentialities due to a lack of freedom. Deprivation may bring about lack of dignity which brings about laziness and unpatriotic behaviors. Unpatriotic behavior usually is a sign of lack of commitment and sense of belonging.

For a country that has seen war like Nigeria; it is wise counsel if it learns to build and reinforce a supportive environment. It is wise counsel if it reinforces competence to strengthen its citizens in the course of which every citizen is led to understand mistakes of the past and the commitment for the present and the vision of the future. One of such competence is sense of belonging.

CHAPTER 4

THE HUMAN CAPITAL RESOURCES/EDUCATION

"Western education which had preceded the British colonial presence combined with growing commercial activities and produced educated and other urban dwellers in the coastal areas of the country. A small educated and politically conscious elite soon emerged in Lagos and other parts of the South. The new elite began to galvanize in the public mind political consciousness, which they utilized to agitate against the colonial administration".[12]

---

[12] Oluwadare Aguda, Understanding the Nigerian Constitution of 1999, (MIJ Publishers Limited 2000) in "Economic and Social Rights: A Century of Constitutional Subordination in Nigeria by Uchechukwu Mgwaba.

The Nigerian education system was supposed to be one of the best; producing great minds and the best educators because the Nigerian learning environment even though hostile and tensed, students still maintain all the possibility and potentiality to learn even in defiance of partly the operant principle of using conditioning of the mind of learners with rewards and punishment in learning. This is because in the Nigerian history of education what we have was the use of punishment to condition and coerce the learner to learn. Nigerian students are ready to learn even without rewards and even in front of punishment; hash weather, poor living condition and hostile teaching methodology. Nigerian students are eager to learn even when they are hungry. With the way the operant principle is applied in education with the use of reward system in most of the top third world countries and even in the first world in order not to produce indolent students or to condition young learners' minds to the enthusiasm of learning; if such system is used in Nigeria even with half measure the Nigerian education system will top the world.

Even in the midst of the unstable system in the education economy of Nigeria; Nigerian students remain consistent in their pursuit of learning. The degree of dedication towards education for Nigerian students is stunning. Nigerian-American achievement in the world of education top all other US immigrant groups.[13]

I remember after the Nigerian Civil War stories had it that children who were of school age were bundled to school with whip. And that many of them underwent all sorts of inhuman treatments in the learning environment; and could you believe that some of them today are the university professors teaching

---

[13] Azu Okon, Feb. 22, 2020 Cowry News and CNN News. https://www.cowrynews.com/data-reveals-nigerians-the-most-educated-in-america-africans-from-the-dark-continent/

in various tertiary institutions. The evidence that Nigeria is a fertile soil for education and learning can be self-revealing.

A great country like the United States of America in 2001 had to make a "U" turn in their education system through introducing a system called "No Child Left Behind" (NCLB). The No Child Left Behind Act is aimed at raising the standard of public primary and secondary education based on students' and teachers' performance through increased accountability and to raise the learners' level of proficiency.

The evidence is self revealing on the behavior of undergraduates, graduates and the Nigerian workforce and in the social sphere the need of dedication toward integral education in order to stand up in defense of values, which is a great reward; but the remote result of the politics of lax conscience has done a great harm to the scheme of education.

The degree of dedication towards education and work in Nigeria has been affected by the unstable economy of Nigeria where there is poor regulation, poor means of information, feed backing and next-to-nothing means of transportation; whereas regularized negotiation and surveillance are usually not regarded as important dimension of diplomacy. Education and the respect for skill and training are derided and ridiculed; based on this backdrop people would remain mentally lazy toward education and work and may consequently develop wrong attitude towards work. And from the outlook of the education process in Nigeria one may see a glaring education systemic source of exploitation rather than source of motivation.

Education must be recognized as a broad social capital that equips people with social competence, interpersonal relationships, shared sense of identity, shared understanding, shared norms, shared values, trust, cooperation, and reciprocity.

According to Will Kenton (2019) in his effort to summarize authors' concept of human capital; "Human capital is an intangible asset or quality not listed on a company's balance sheet. It can be classified as the economic value of a worker's experience and skills or the value of human capacities. This includes assets like education, training, intelligence, skills, health, and other things employers value such as loyalty and punctuality".

A person's economy of life is his aggregation of achievement. It is the composite of his education, training, skill, experience, exposure and vigorous imagination. As a personal asset it is a person's life-time investment.

The aggregation of a person's intangible value has economic benefit for the individual and the State. So how does government contribute in adding to the value of the citizens' intangible assets of education, training, experience and skill? This part of the paper tries to analyze the concept of human capital in Nigeria in terms of education using the following critical outlines:

- Regulation – order - controls
- Information - knowledge
- Negotiation – diplomacy
- Surveillance - supervision

How do Nigerian teachers and professors apply regulation and order in their work? How best are they equipped for the work? Work is more a pleasure and satisfying if a worker knows his work, feels satisfied doing it; that means s/he has the right skill for the job. "The best way not to feel hopeless is to get up and do something – do some work. Do not wait for good things to happen on their own accord. If you go out and make some good things happen, you will fill the world with hope, you will fill yourself with hope." (Barack Obama).

Proper regulation, information, negotiation and surveillance promote the value of the human capital. Investing in human capital through proper regulation, information, negotiation and surveillance give citizens of a country opportunity to participate effectively in the socio-political activities of the country with and in their best human assets.

The asset of human investment is the only direct recourse toward diversification in business, creating jobs, creating products and services. The countries that invest highly in human assets have greater asset of human capital, innovative economy; competitive environment and collaborative effort. Such countries spend a great portion of their revenue in providing means to regularize and control their citizens' human asset contribution. Such countries often witness long term stability in their economy. A successful economy depicts educated, intelligent and skillful people who make up the greater portion of the knowledgeable population. "We often miss opportunity because it's dressed in overalls and looks like work" (Thomas A. Edison). Nigerian socio-economic model has yet to recognize the value of education, the value of work, the right, diplomacy and respect to work; which is why private owners of places of work exploit and trifle with the emotions time and interest of their workers.

The idea of human capital is based on the principle of unequal labor force or inequality of labor (Will Kenton 2019). But the concept of human capital has come a long way through the study of human resources management, business management and macroeconomics. The human capital history can be traced back to Adam Smith, Arthur Lewis, Arthur Cecil Pigou, Gary Becker, Jacob Mincer and Theodore Schultz etc. The authors said supposedly that citizens and workers need to be provided with means to improve their status of work by gaining higher education, training and exposure; all happen for the name of higher standard of life, value, national prestige and stable and competitive economy as one of the principle which forms the basis of socio-political and socio-economic activity of great countries.

The degree of dedication towards work in an unstable economy like Nigeria where there is poor regulation, poor attitude toward information and dilapidated means of transportation, poor negotiation and surveillance will usually amount to nothing because the work satisfaction is lacking. Such reflects the degree to which Nigerian workers are bored hence they need restructuring of the system and motivation. Nigerian citizens who were ready to work in the labor market are exposed to so many awkward situations in the name of work because of lack of regulation and negotiation. Regulation and negotiation need to be reviewed.

Even if the proportion of the skilled, effective and dedicated workers may remain very high as it is in Nigeria; the economy vis-a-vis the aggregation of human capital would still remain bored and slow. Poverty level would remain spiraling and exponentially high. In such economic situation where there is poor regulation, surveillance and negotiation foreign industries prefer to hire foreign labor as it is the case with most of the foreign industries in Nigeria.

The system in Nigeria still remains highly exploitative as a result of lack of diplomacy, regulation and negotiation. And even if there were regulation it is better in theory than in practice. And if that is the case; negotiation would be meaningless. One of the remedies would be to make the hiring industries conformable to regulation. Another would be to implement categorization whereby industries are involved with the subsidizing of training whereby they can train local skills or subsidize the cost of training of local skills. In this way indigenous and foreign industries are involved in the trade-off to raise the standard of training in order to move quickly into high-tech productivity, manufacturing and services by enforcing regulation, improved attitude toward information, negotiation and supervision with dedication to build the country and the economy.

Proper enforcement of regulation is congrurnt with proper negotiation and both would protect the up-coming industries. And through less tax the up-coming industries would be enabled to grow and to ensure they abide by the rules of employment; by this Nigerian economy will ramp and Nigeria as a nation would truly belong to one of the fastest developing economies of the world through making educational industries priority.

Difficulties that Need Serious Attention in Nigerian Education

- Parental and family difficulties
- School environment and teacher preparation difficulties
- Student self-imposed difficulties
- The uninvolved, self-willed-child difficulties
- Insufficient instruction difficulties

What are the parental and family difficulties in the Nigerian educational setting? Some parents are bent on over-exploiting their children all in the name of the Nigerian rough economy. This is difficulty set on by financial situation. As a result the child had no time neither of his/her own nor time to study and they expect miracles to happen concerning the academic ability of the child. Some parents are not aware of their child's academic challenges. This difficulty is set on by something far from financial situation. Such child needs personal attention different or similar to an uninvolved child. Parents not being aware of the developmental challenges of the child may pose great difficulties to a child's learning ability. These are the parental and family difficulties that might hinder the learning progress of a child. A good education governance and management must build a system of support and opportunity that attacks parents' and family impediments to student success.

What are the school environment and teachers' difficulties that may frustrate a child's academic progress? There is increasing agreement between educators and researchers that teachers' attitude and learning environment affect students' academic performance. (Cf. The Research Alliance for New York City Schools 2016). The study showed that:

"Learning environments play a significant role in student success. Most educators have suspected this for decades, and now they have evidence showing that schools can potentially lift student achievement by improving their learning environments. We show that improvements in the school context within a school over time are associated with corresponding increases in student achievement gains,"

These results further illustrate the importance of both individual and organizational effectiveness when designing reforms aimed at raising student achievement. (Cf. The Research Alliance for New York City Schools, School Organizational Contexts, Teacher Turnover, and Student Achievement: Mathew A. Kraft-Brown University, William H. Marinell, Darrick Yee-Harvard University. March 2016).

Students' Progress and Adversity Quotient (2016): A research conducted in Manila used as a reference point in the PhD Dissertation of Dr. Basil Onyejuruwa. The research investigated on students' achievement and how the character of teachers and managers becomes the factor to students' fulfillment. The consequences of this study confirmed that scholars attained higher fulfillment scores in faculties with higher adversity quotient principals and managers.

What is the Student self-imposed difficulty that may hinder a student's academic progress? It makes great sense perhaps to introduce learners to ways they can appreciate that education is the means to lead them out of their self-imposed limitations ab initio. Etymologically from the French language educare stands for education; the combination of the letter or word as the case may be 'e' with 'ducare'; the first means 'out' and the second means 'lead', the combination implies 'to lead out' or to draw out. It could also mean to draw out the best in a person in order for s/he to face difficulties. Self-imposed difficulties may be seen in most specific ways playing out in a child in the attitude of uninvolved, careless or care free, unconscious or unaware of reality and sometimes self-willed. These are fetters of iron and shackles on the image of the person which the person does not see; only the good teacher can draw the person out of these and gradually re-impose the required standards. The Leverage this book is offering for the difficulties that need serious attention in Nigerian education is for a good school governance and management.

INTEGRAL EDUCATION IN NIGERIA

What is the education for integral human person for? What are the essential features for integral education? What are the ideological and conceptual frameworks? What is the paradigm shifts from other educational systems? What are the pedagogical practices consistent with integral learning system? (It is less than teacher centered and greater than student centered; it is teaching learning and holistic achievement centered). What type of school organization and condition that would favor it? What types of school and community partnerships are required for it?

Integral education and insufficient instruction seem like two parallel lines that can never meet. Integral education depends very much on the type of organized instruction and the aim and the impact being for integral development of the human person. Teachers should be prepared with the impact of integral education.

Insufficient instruction is an act of impacting education in a haphazard way implying lack of preparedness, and lack of in-depth knowledge and lack of concern to the aim of education. According to Jean Piaget "the first task of the educator is to generate interest". And for him the main aim of education is:

> "The creation of men and women who are capable of doing new things, not simply repeating what other generations have done. Men and women who are creative, inventive and discoverers. People who can be ctitical, validating, and not necessarily accepting everything that is offered to them".

There is a new wave of standards in education reform. It is a new standard which makes education greatly accountable and as a result instruction is made integral in education. Instruction is all that matters in integral education; not just any how instruction but effective and high quality and proficient instruction; which for Harvard's Public Education Leadership Program has called *instructional core*. "It was no longer acceptable to simply deliver instruction and either the students got it, or they didn't and then regardless, the teacher just moved on". (Paul Reville 2017). Teachers' training should be prepared towards making students realize their full academic and educational potential, as the goal of integral education.

The Nigerian society is characterized by growing inequality with observable diminishing social mobility together with human capital – knowledge and skills, social capital (competence) – learning opportunities, (experience); these are the fundamentals of integral human capital.

Integral education takes place with the essential element of education, or integral education is fostered by means of the essential elements of education:

- The Teacher – pedagogical skill
- The Curriculum with general goal of education and specifics
- Conventional knowledge critical and adventurous

- Personal awareness of Academic ability; for a learner to be confident that s/he is capable of learning things
- Value knowledge - Mores – standards
- Formation and outcome based - cognitive, affective and psychomotor domain making the learner greatly versatile

Transformational education or integral education system has a role to play in the reform of Nigerian education. The rationale for talking about integral teaching and learning is to draw out the best in the practices of teaching and learning with richer content, core competences with habits of the mind in such a way that students be part of what they have learned and participate actively in social actions of the future.

It is a complete teaching and learning system that equip teachers and students with the right way of thinking and looking at the society, achieving economic prosperity and producing responsible citizenship. Integral teaching and learning draw out the best from the role of teaching and learning in order to shape the future that everybody desires.

According to Pope Paul VI, the development of peoples must be well rounded; it must foster the development of each man and of the whole man.[14]

In his Encyclical Letter *Populorum Progressio* of 1967, the Holy Father explains his ideas concerning integral human development or education as:

> "A vocation that needs development in God's plan; every man is born to seek self-fulfillment because every human life is called to some task by God. At birth a human being possesses certain aptitudes and abilities in germinal form, and these qualities are to be cultivated so that they may bear fruit. By developing these traits through formal education of personal effort, the individual works his way toward the goal set for him by the Creator. Endowed with intellect and free will, each man is responsible for his self-fulfillment even as he is for his salvation. He is helped, and sometimes hindered, by his teachers and those around him; yet whatever be the outside influences exerted on him, he is the chief architect of his own success or failure. Utilizing only his talent and willpower, each man can grow in humanity, enhance his personal worth, and perfect himself".[15]

---

[14] Pope Paul VI, Populorum Progressio n. 14, 1967 (Integral Human Development)

The Pope further explains that each *individual belongs to a community and must participate in the community duties:*

> "Self-development, however, is not left up to man's option. Just as the whole of creation is ordered toward its Creator, so too the rational creature should of his own accord direct his life to God, the first truth and the highest good. Thus human self-fulfillment may be said to sum up our obligations. Moreover, this harmonious integration of our human nature, carried through by personal effort and responsible activity, is destined for a higher state of perfection. United with the life-giving Christ, man's life is newly enhanced; it acquires a transcendent humanism which surpasses its nature and bestows new fullness of life. This is the highest goal of human self-fulfillment. Each man is also a member of society; hence he belongs to the community of man. It is not just certain individuals but all men who are called to further the development of human society as a whole. Civilizations spring up, flourish and die. As the waves of the sea gradually creeps farther and farther in along the shoreline, so the human race inches its way forward through history. We are the heirs of earlier generations, and we reap benefits from the efforts of our contemporaries; we are under obligation to all men. Therefore, we cannot disregard the welfare of those who will come after us to increase the human family. The reality of human solidarity brings us not only benefits but also obligations …".[16]

---

[15] Ibid n. 15
[16] Ibid n. 16 & 17

From the theoretical point of view, integral education is not a philosophy of education or a principle either; but it is a process of achieving the aim of education through drawing on different effective methodologies of teaching and learning in making the teacher educator and the learner integral part of what is learned which educators have used even in disguise. It is the rationale and understanding behind every piece of learning. Take for instance, according to Rebecca Ray concerning the rationale of UBD: "*Understanding By Design*, or *UBD*, is a framework and accompanying design process for thinking decisively about unit lesson planning. The concept was developed by Jay McTighe and Grant Wiggins, and as part of their principles they state that UBD "…is not a philosophy of education". It is not designed to tell teachers what or how to teach; it is a system to help them teach more effectively. In fact, its flexibility is one reason it has gained so much acclaim. With UBD, the ultimate goal is to think backward, focusing on the big picture: at the end of a unit what is the essential question your students should be able to answer"?

Integral education obtains a pedagogical system or process supported by constructive reasoning breaking learning in pieces whereby each piece of learning is used in demonstrating the relational appropriateness which corresponds with the ultimate meaning of teaching and learning desires. Since each piece of knowledge has aim(s); the teacher and the learner equally must have the desire to meet with such aim(s) for the integrity of teaching and learning to

---

[17] Holistic education is a relatively new movement in education that seeks to engage all aspects of the learner, including mind, body, and spirit. Its philosophy, which is also identified as holistic learning theory, is based on the premise that each person finds identity, meaning, and purpose in life through connections to their local community, to the natural world, and to humanitarian values such as compassion and peace. Holistic education aims to call forth from people an intrinsic reverence for life and a passionate love of learning, gives attention to experiential learning, and places significance on " relationships and primary human values within the learning environment". The term "holistic education" is most often used to refer to the more democratic and humanistic types of alternative education.

be accomplished. Integral teaching and learning must play one of the leading roles in attacking the diminishing desire of teaching and learning in Nigerian education and as one of the great challenges of global education success. Integral education is a form of holistic education.[17] Integral education consists from a love of learning; from the Greek word "Philomath" means love of "learning" and studying (the process of gaining or acquiring knowledge). This is quite different from the word "Philosophy" which means love of "wisdom" or love of "knowledge". Integral education inspires experiential learning (EXL); this is the method of learning by experience which is precisely described as learning through reflection and doing. It is not totally hands-on learning because students do not reflect on their "doing" in hands-on learning. And EXL is different also from didactic learning where learners play passive role in the process. It is perhaps similar to other ways of learning like: adventure learning, action learning, cooperative learning, free-choice learning, situated learning and service learning.

The origin of holistic education is connected with the beginning of the idea of instruction in the ancient Greece and other cultures.[18] It precisely focuses on the learning method which emphasizes the whole aspects of a person and not just a dimension of the individual's experience; and this eventually formed the view that the whole world is one single reality hence the catalyst for man's quest for learning. And that learning cannot be separated from man's experiences or that

---

[18] *Geri, Salinitri (2020), Handbook of Research on Leadership Experience for Academic Direction (LEAD) Programs for Student Success. Hershey, PA: IGI Global. p. 227. ISBN 978-1-7998-2431-2.*

[19] *Alfred Adler was an Austrian medical doctor, psychotherapist and founder of the school of individual psychology. His emphasis on the importance of feelings of inferiority, the inferiority complex, is recognized as an isolating element which plays a key role in personality development. Alfred Adler considered a human being as an individual whole, therefore he called his psychology "Individual Psychology".*

man is synonymous with his learning experiences. In this way; learning becomes the integrity of man. Hence this book emphasizes the usefulness of integral education.

This idea was in part framed from Alfred Adler's concept of "individual psychology", in which he sees a human being as an individual whole.[19] Integral education would impact students in the following ways:

- It would improve students' learning and attitudes towards learning
- It would lead students to improve their behavior towards reality
- Students would form the habit to seek for what unites one piece of knowledge with another
- Students would be more confident with life because they can gain greater knowledge of reality
- They would be able to analyze between education and life

- Students would become more aware of the needs of their community
- Students would appreciate to be part of the civic duties and gain more mastery of the environmental challenges
- Students would become more active in matters of well-being, risk taking and safety.

Teachers would exhibit:

- More mutual support for one another in order to achieve greater academic success for their students
- More skills behaviorally and attitudinally for effective school management
- More attitude of sacrifice and perseverance in behalf of the students

The community would:

- Perceive a whole school culture on the environment
- Perceive more meaningful relationship between parents and the school and community

- Encourage students and teachers' health through supports for medical care and social needs
- Promote actions and behaviors that encourage values and better living

Integral education for a prosperous future manned by educators who are the most influential change agents in modeling is necessary for educational reform in Nigeria.

Integral education and the fundamental value of learning are congruent with the universality of learning; all men desire to know beginning from the least to that which leads to the totality

---

[20] *The Affluent Society* is a 1958 book by Harvard economist John Kenneth Galbraith. The book sought to clearly outline the manner in which the post–World War II United States was becoming wealthy in the private sector but remained poor in the public sector, lacking social and physical infrastructure, and perpetuating income disparities. The book sparked much public discussion at the time. It is also credited with popularizing the term "conventional wisdom". Many of the ideas presented were later expanded and refined in Galbraith's 1967 book, *The New Industrial State*.

in the significant unity. It makes learning the integral part of life. Integral education in its kind of pedagogy is transformative. Reforming and modeling, it promotes proficiency of skill and peoples' way of thinking, this means using modern ideas and technology in the most dynamic, pragmatic and effective ways in order to benefit greatly on what John Kenneth Galbraith calls conventional wisdom.[20] Such are those commonplace beliefs that are also acceptable and comfortable to society, which can be applied thus enhancing their ability to resist facts that might diminish them or diminish human integrity.

According to a data provided by Rice University in Texas, Nigerian-Americans are the most educated "ethnic" group in the United States. Although they represent a tiny portion of the U.S population, est, 380,000, 37% of them hold a bachelor's degree, 17% a master's while 29% age 25 and above possess a graduate degree compared to 11% of the US population.

Nigerians account for less than 1 percent of the American population but shockingly make up 25% of all the black students at Harvard Business School. It then comes as no surprise that the Nigerian-American achievement in the world of education top all other US immigrant groups. (Cf. Azu Okon, Feb. 22, 2020 Cowry News and CNN News. https://www.cowrynews.com/data-reveals-nigerians-the-most-educated-in-america-africans-from-the-dark-continent/).

Why is it that Nigeria has more educated people than some of the greatly prosperous world? Why is Nigeria social-political order lags in global standards? People become more educated society and proficient, dedicated, effective, creative, innovative and flexible, committed and ready to shine when they have education supported by integral human development. Nigeria needs to transform her basic political and governing will and make her education system work for the good of the future then Nigerians in diaspora would do well to go home and invest their capital and talents with confidence and peace of mind. These suggest that there must be a win-win conflict resolution conference in Nigeria among the integrally educated Nigerians to achieve standards based economy and education and balance of power where sense of belonging produces genuine respect for one another.

Nigerians who were fortunate to go abroad, studied abroad and got exposed may have seen what is lacking in the Nigerian context and probably are aware of what needs to be done to fix it; such people have real fear concerning the level of impunity in the use of military to destabilize thought leaders and those with genuine spirit of sacrifice.

Upon reflecting on the statistics on how Nigerian citizens play leading role in educational pursuit and achievement in United State, one would understand through deductive reasoning that Nigerians are greatly gifted and talented and cannot be pushed over in any aspect of global competition. Nigerian brains are scattered in every fields of learning in different universities in every part of the world. They like to remain with the environment that recognizes and respect the role they play in integral human development for the country.

The Nigerian elementary and secondary education what reforms and modification may be enforced as approaches for integral learning? For instance lack of effectiveness in communicating to children sense of community civic responsibility and social skills that reflect the profile of chronological age – gender - and in specific context and in general expectations; "The expectations for people to behave appropriately form the foundation for a society" (Berns, 2013). Many of life's social expectations are made clear and enforced on a cultural level. John Locke, an English philosopher regarded the minds of new born babies as a tabula rasa and a blank slate upon which life experiences and the society writes its norms and values and possible expectations. Socialization hence becomes the process through which children acquire societal norms, values, habits, ideals, and expectations.

Because socialization is passed on from generation to generation, a generation must not fail the next in passing on the right values because the effects if not done or done haphazardly are grave. It is therefore important for these socializing agents and other individuals who work with these children to recognize and be sensitive to their physical, psychological, and social needs and provide supportive and nurturing experiences for the children in homes, schools, religious centers, and other public places. (Ajayi, J.O., & Owumi, B. 2013).

Much effort may be required to reform teaching and learning methods in order to align with integral development. To communicate integral education takes a teacher who has the best of intention, skills and proficiency towards learning and learners; such leader would light followers up rather than burn them out. That caliber of a leader is very important today to raise the environment of learning. It is only a passionate leader that can initiate the integral approaches.

Nigeria needs a reform in education; there is strong correlation between high achievements in learners with the attitude of the teacher towards teaching and learning. Nigeria needs integrally developed leaders, students and explorers with high enthusiasm and charisma. Such are the model of leaders who can motivate such dry environment like Africa for the hungry and the weak, the sick and the dry-bone, the angry and the sober, the abnormal and the normal. Such leaders will bring back Africans to their home where they were once prosperous and inspired by adventure that open the doors for the world's invention and the beginning of every education with boundless possibilities and infinite accomplishment. These are the leaders that will transform Africa. Long have Africa been producing leaders who were busy doing so much but achieving nothing; long have African leaders been led by their counterparts across the sea and deceived by the pictures of the colors of the moons and the rainbows and led them back home with frustration. Long have African leaders been made to feel that they cannot compete in the global circle. Transformational and integral leaders know that life is the same from the east to the west and from the north to the south and interconnected and that there is no reality visible or invisible that contributes nothing to the human world, just as every African must contribute to the reality of Africa. A real leader is altruistic, integrally developed and courageous not because he/she inherited the traits but because he/she developed the skills through love of learning.

A real leader does not isolate any paradigm or principle, concept, conceit or mindset. He/she does not allow the potentials of the future to be subsumed in the big-picture. The transforming skill of an integral leader approaches life new every day. He/she knows the value of intense preparation for each new day and how to begin each day with the end in mind or how to end each day without avoiding tomorrow.

Education and Skilled Labor

Skilled labor requires high education and training following the concept of unequal labor (Will Kenton 2019). The demand for skilled labor by industries supposedly is the result of globalization. Skilled labor is expensive apparently but settling with unskilled labor has long term drawback. This is one reason that Nigeria has faced which makes education reform most crucial. According to Adam Smith, the increasing human capital and industrial development play a great role in the global strong factor in deciding the level of economy of a country. In Eamonn Butler's comments on Adam Smith's book "The Wealth of Nations" he mentioned that "the countries that prosper are those that grow their capital, manage it well, and protect it". The human capital in Adam Smith's Wealth of Nations includes education for the most part which is the catalyst for skilled labor.

Comparative advantage may draw industries with variety of advantages together in favor of an economy all things being equal. Effective labor force boosts the economy of a country but when these labor forces are concentrated on a particular region diminishing value may soon set in and comparative advantage may become comparative disadvantage.

The economy of a country reflects the quality of its education and the quality of its workforce. A rich country has the quality of workforce that is able to serve in her industries in a way that such country maintains a high comparative advantage and competitive advantage in very many productive capacities and stable economy than other countries.

There are many countries producing millions of barrels of crude oil in a day that depended on the more civilized countries to refine their crude oil and sometimes they end up buying the refined oil much expensive compared to the crude oil which they sold to those countries where the crude oil was being refined.

Some of these great oil producing countries have similar economic disadvantages; first is that the leaders do not have a better altruistic integrated thinking capacity as well as a team of committed workforce to run their oil industries where the crude oil may be refined. They chose the easy way out to sell their crude oil and later buy it as refined oil with much taxes and international trade rules. As mal-practicing leaders they chose short term benefits.

Crude oil industry is just one of the many industries in some of the so-called third-world countries where such impediment inheres. The banking industries, the hospital institutions and the construction careers, including automobile producing industries in some of the third-world countries are impeded because of the limiting self-centeredness and lack of integrated thinking ability. The consequences are poor commitment, embarking on short term goals, lack of trust and gross indiscipline.

The sacrifice needed in order to raise the standard of leadership, commitment and competence may be enormous as it involves education reform, thinking habit and character; the benefits may make a nation greater than the cost. "Education is the most powerful instrument which you can use to change the world" (Nelson Mandela). Though education is "expensive" but ignorance is doubly misery. "The function of education is to teach one to think intensively and to think critically. Intelligence plus character - that is the goal of true education" (Martin Luther King, Jr.).

The incentive needed so as to raise the standard of commitment to teaching and learning includes:

- Subsidizing educational tuition fees

- Motivational aids to keep children in love with learning

- More qualified teachers should teach out of passion and satisfaction rather than for money…

- Free recreational facilities to improve leisure, health of mind and body

- Easy learning aids/instructional aids

- Reintroduce learning as a pleasure not as a task or punishment

- Developing the mind and skill through benchmarking integral learning

Education is a global challenge. Developing countries are mustering resources to develop educational standard that would produce the workforce that would be able to deliver the skill and mindset needed to run their industries and improve their economy.

A viable education system is an investment. Nigeria economy would grow greater if the education system is improved. Citizens of Nigeria must learn that a strong economy is the result of workers who pull their human resources and intellectual skill voluntarily together toward such purpose as patriotic service. A viable education system produces efficient workers.

A viable education system must produce the skill of critical thinking and committed work habit. And as the proportion of such committed workers grow so the economy of the country exponentially grows. Subsidizing or funding the primary and secondary education becomes not a novel in the contemporary economy of Nigeria but a long standing project as a long term vision to transform the country's industrial ability, economic growth and stability and performance.

The education quality of Nigeria must be the leverage to compete with other countries. It is the Nigerian human capital and human resources across the globe compared to other countries. In every economy where there is increase of skilled labor supply in proportion to increase in industrial demand with honest supervision and regulatory controls wage standard may not fall or even be compromised. Such large scale production of skilled labor becomes a source of international exchange. A practical example is the Philippines with its large scale production of skilled labor and professional workers, which forms the greatest source of the countries international exchange. The opposite may be the case where there is an increase in the number of graduates in disproportion with the number of industries and there is no proper diplomacy to exchange such huge number of graduates at the international market; and that would end up like lose to the economy until a reform is established.

Such disproportion carries along it so many psycho-social viruses like; when young people are fed with the idea that "why do you have to go to school when you cannot have a job to practice the skill you have studied"? This is the concept of the Nigerian education. That is the concept which has conceited the mind of young people and even most professors such that educational programs in Nigeria were drawn with laissez-faire; a situation where people approach education with mere quid pro quo. It is education that lacks quiddity; education in-a-hurry and education under fear.

Federalizing Nigeria will be a great advantage towards industrializing Nigeria and would be a great advantage to the educational industry as each state would concentrate on how better to develop its system.

Federalizing Nigeria will unearth many loopholes which have been swept under the carpet; that is it would open Nigerian hard-working people to consider the gap between Nigeria as a developing country with other developed world; so then the competition would begin first, by considering how to provide the level ground for Nigerian citizens to measure up with their counterparts across the globe. Not federalizing Nigeria has hidden so many loopholes in the crowd of noise. Long have people been taught that "two or many heads are better than one"; meaning that "crowd is better than few" but lately experience has shown that "one good head is better than many". Nigeria is the giant of Africa; giant may not merely be about her population size; otherwise it may mean a "crowd". Giant should be on their ability to stand out as good example in governance by approaching and accessing the modern and the most plausible and pragmatic system of governance.

VALUES, LIFE STYLE AND SOCIAL AFFAIRS – EDUCATION MATTERS

The global education culture matters in values learning. Or values learning matters in the global education culture.

The Nigerian education curriculum would do more to engage learners understanding, attitudes, lifestyle and ability to judge social matters through values learning as a means to communicate what the society prioritized as important and ideal behavior which would help students exhibit better citizenship and contribute to the resources of the Nation. Character education, moral education, ethical learning is the implication of proper understanding of the ideals of an environment. If students would learn more of the social affairs and history of their past and make such learning experiences a guide to the future; their attitude towards learning and love to the country would improve. Values like fairness, social justice, trust, kindness, respect and responsibility etc, must be reconsidered as part of social strategies of education to rebuild the falling Nigerian ideals. Educators agree that those behaviors can be communicated, learned and developed through making it a series of pedagogies to improve integral learning on people who are capable of acting ethically, for social cohesion, responsibility, trustworthy, respect for ideals and ready to sacrifice. Through these the country can reshape the people's mind concerning ethnic difference, religious affiliation and tribal self-interest. There is no greater awareness about social values for Nigerians now than the learning experience of the past and the values of sense of belonging and communal efforts to improve the failed leadership and failed learning habit. Nigerian education system would produce students who learned from the combination with spiritual maturity and academic and social balance; people who are competent, reliable, who have conscience and compassion. That is what it would be with professional and transformative thinking leaders who would not be afraid to stand up for integrity and for inclusion. Nigerians have come from different backgrounds and they want to work toward common goals. This would be the assignment of wider network of pedagogical and social strategy for new education structure at this time. Some education leaders have in the past paid lip service to these values; those who continue that way would be removed from the system. This book is challenging readers to make a longitudinal observation of all the past Nigerian leaders' achievements, attitudinal or relational behavior concerning all the mentioned patriotic values in this book and evaluate which leader actually worked for the common goals. Let the Nigerian education system be challenged that there is still very much to be done to roll out educational pragmatic curriculum that would produce people of sound understanding of social cohesion, critical thinking and smart decision making ability who can foresee the future rather than being obstacle for the future.

Perennial Agitation: Learning Experience

Time and again there had always been ethnic confrontation among the Igbo people, Hausa people and Yoruba which took a significant number of lives. The first of this unrest happened in Jos between 1932 and 1945.

> "A recurring national dilemma: violent rioting. This phenomenon has become a fun house in Nigeria and is often callously executed with deep-seated hatred, crammed with religious, tribal, ethnic and regional colorations" (Ephraim Adinlofu Feb. 4 2009).

It erupted in an undertone of the Southerners domination of Jos and its environs. The Jos riot of 1945 by the Beroms and the Hausas according to E. Adinlofu is a recurring phenomenon which has presented a historical dimension of the ugly side of Nigeria.

An antecedent to 1945 was an ethnic uprising of 1932 between the Hausa settlers in Jos and the indigenes of Jos which simmered up to the struggle that triggered the Jos riot of 1945. According to record the insurrection happened within the fleet of two days in which more than 300 Igbo people died and many people were injured. It was known that the riot of 1945 happened as a result of the general strike action which was understood to be initiated by the Igbo against the British rule. Since the Hausa nevertheless compromised with the British colonial rule; the uprising came however being instigation by the British on the Hausa against the Igbo. A lesson on the seed of discrimination sown by the ideological prejudice and bias of British to be learned but does not seem as learned. The lesson is that 'you (Igbo, Hausa and Yoruba) could not learn to coexist with your neighbor and why will you expect a foreigner to strike a deal for your peaceful coexistence with your neighbor.' And even if a foreigner does it for you it will not be a lasting peace; so you should do it among yourselves.

Kano Riot of 1953

This was understood to have started as a result of the controversies on the matters concerning the upcoming independence in 1956. It was understood that the deal was not amenable with the Hausa-Fulani group who rather wanted the British indirect rule to perpetuate longer.

The agitation reached its heights with the leaders of the south and the north in which confrontation ensued and the Igbo suffered the effect with many deaths and lose of properties because they wield economic and social influence on the territory. The four days insurgence took over thirty lives and over two hundred and forty people were injured.

In 1953 Mallam Inua Wada belonged to the party of NPC planned a hostile confrontation against Chief S. L. Akintola of the party of AG who was being expected to arrive in Kano.

The following were the words of Mallam Inua Wada:

"Having abused us in the South, these very Southerners have decided to come over to the North to abuse us, but we are determined to retaliate treatment given to us in the South. We have therefore organized about 1000 men ready in the city to meet force with force. We are determined to show Akintola and his group what we can do in our land when they come… The NPC has declared a strike in all Native Administration offices for Saturday, 16 May 1953… We shall post sufficient number of men at the entrance of every office and business place… We are prepared to face anything that comes out of this business". (Cf. Justice G.C.M Onyiuke Tribunal of Inquiry, titled "MASSACRE OF NDI-IGBO" in 1966).

It was later found out that the retaliation Mallam Wada was referring to which took many lives of many Southerners especially the Igbo was booing and jeering at the Northern members of the parliament during their visit to Lagos.

Justice Onyiuke's remarks captures the fact that public security agents who were supposed to be the Government machinery for peace keeping were conversely used to perpetuate evil. Politicization of the police and the security agents in Nigeria has a long negative history:

"The use of government machinery to perpetuate and escalate the dastardly act. The Native Authority agents, who were supposed to protect the people, became agents of death". (Onyiuke).

The entire Nigerian environment is a flicker of agitation. Agitation is part of peoples' demonstration of democratic and human rights and yearning of the people against poverty, marginalization and absence of opportunity, presence of violence, historic learning failure and leadership failure. "But Nigeria remains haunted by the ghosts of its civil war. It simply stopped the war without addressing its root causes. And by refusing to discuss the war's legacies, the country's rulers bred a deep, dangerous disenchantment" (Max Siollun 2020).

"Therefore, one can relate to the continuous growth in the numbers of Nigeria-Biafra war narratives as a call on the Federal Government of Nigeria never to forget the reasons for the war" (Rantimi Jays Julius-Adeoye 2017).

The Geographical Portion Called the Northern Nigeria

Since self-rule was imminent the British diplomacy in the precaution and concern for the Northerners divided the country into three regions giving the North a big share of the country's geographical proportion. Since the Igbo and the Yoruba elites were desperate to obtain independence there was no room for them to agitate for the clear majority of the geographical section given to the North.

The Yoruba and the Igbo groups; the AG and the NCNC once had Lagos for "tug of war". The AG reiterated that Lagos belongs to the Western Nigeria and must be understood as Yoruba territory. The NCNC protested that Lagos should be known as a "no man's land". The agitation led the Yoruba group to declare support to the country in building another capital territory in any part of Nigeria so long as Lagos must be known and recognized as a Yoruba land. Against this the Yoruba groups threatened to secede from Nigeria if Lagos ceases to be recognized as Yoruba land and this was recorded as the first attempt to secede from Nigeria. These events were recorded as part of the 1950's immediately preceding the independence.

The First Threat of Secession from the West

The first threat made by the Yoruba group by the AG to secede from Nigeria persisted with a demand that the right to secede from the country by any part of Nigeria be incorporated in the constitution in case such people have convincing reasons and need for that. This was later discussed in the Constitutional Conference convened in 1954 in London.

The NCNC argued against the proposal to enshrine in the constitution of the emerging independent Nigeria with reasons that the clause with the right of secession would not benefit the unity of the entire emerging nation with the unitary pattern of governance and that the provision for right of secession in the constitution would likely mar the structure of a unitary system of governance.

NCNC was later joined with the NPC against the heated agitation to include the clause for right of secession in the constitution by the AG in which case the British gave backing and lobbied for the support of the NCNC and the NPC and warned that the Great Britain might take the agitation of the AG for secession as treasonable act. Based on this back drop the AG was forced to withdraw their agitation to include the right to secede as part of the constitution.

One can argue that if the clause for the right of secession was enshrined in the early Nigerian constitution it would have been unnecessary for the Biafran Nigerian war to happen in 1967 fourteen years later. One can see from here how Nigerian early leaders acquired western education, besides remain good illiterates, uniformed and untaught. These can say volume about the Nigerian elites who first acquired the western education; they were by far apart from the vision upon which the structural, social and physical development of the country was founded. Instead of being pioneers of blessing and light they were pioneers of tribalism, ethnic and cultural exclusionism.

None of these parties even with their education knew they were building on a wrong foundation and motivation in preparation for the emerging self-rule country. It could hardly be read through a microscope that the alliance between the NCNC and the NPC before independence was the factor to determine the spurious future of the country in many perspectives. That is the hidden hand of British on the self-rule.

THE NIGERIAN SOCIO-ECONOMIC AFFAIRS

Socioeconomics or social economics is about how to use the knowledge of social process to improve economic affairs and how to integrate economic affairs with social life of a people. Social thinkers are people of visionary for the advancement of society; they are perceived as visionaries who chart the courses of development with the best forecast of the future for the society.

By trying to think socially and economically people process how their thoughts, feelings and intention and behavior make sense along with other people's thoughts and actions in the context of interacting with one another in the society. It is about the relation of economics to social values. It features the reciprocal relationship between economic science and social philosophy-ethical science or human dignity in the process of reconstructing education for a better society and advancement. This element of knowledge is put far behind by many business moguls of Nigeria who practice the shrewdest attitude with a pound of flesh in their business enterprises. In fact due to global backdrop social context of individuals and interactions and experiences have triple phases: the social and economic which influence the degree to which individuals can improve their abilities and realize their potentials and the language to communicate.

More than 75 years ago George Mead (1934), a social interaction theorist, wrote that it is language that sharply separates humans from other animals. Let us use English language for a practical example here. England has English language as the major factor on their political and economic superiority over other countries as their patent exclusive found and invention and they claim right of ownership especially in every setting where the language is used as a means of interaction etc. This particular language has blossomed due to the common use; almost English is becoming the number one language in every part of the world. In fact thinkers cite that it was this very fact that has placed the United Kingdom on a superior economic height over other countries.

Mead goes on to say that language makes ideas and communication of people's ideas possible, and language also makes it possible to replace action with thoughts and then use thoughts to transform behavior. Imagine how beautiful the ethnic languages and dialects in Nigeria are; these are the means of communication and medium of thinking. Socialization is how Nigerians learn the norms and beliefs of Nigerian society. Through the languages that are spoken in Nigeria and by the importance educational advancement made of them; the people would became increasingly aware of the social and economic values and expectations of the society.

Socialization is the process through which people are taught to be proficient members of a society. It describes the ways that people come to understand societal norms and expectations and to accept what the society teaches and beliefs, and to be familiar with the societal values. Socialization is how people learn the norms and beliefs – the does and don'ts of society. "While socialization enables a person to participate in social groups and society, it also enables the very existence of a society and its consequent social order" (Berns, 2013). This book is challenging Nigerian society for being part of the failure of itself for lack of the use of genuine socializing units with systems, conferences, educational organizations and social discussions.

Social thinking tries to assess whether people are actively interacting or fighting it out. Social thinking is a competence and ability by which people process and store information of the past and uses it for the advancement of the future. It is a social competence and ability to process and store information about people and social situations, apply the information in the most positive ways to further social interactions, common idea and relationship.

Nigerian educators and education system still have a long way to go with regards to social skills. Looking at the way people posit their agitation against the government or against a group and the way the government process agitations will testify the truth that social skills in the Nigerian education system is still a long way backward.

"Social competence consists of social, emotional, cognitive and behavioral skills needed for successful social adaptation. Social competence also reflects having an ability to take another's perspective concerning a situation, learn from past experiences, and apply that learning to the changes in social interactions." Semrud Clikeman, M. (2007).

"Social competence is the foundation upon which expectations for future interaction with others are built, and upon which individuals develop perceptions of their own behavior. Social competence frequently encompasses social skills, social communication, and interpersonal communication." Semrud Clikeman, M. (2007).

EDUCATION AND SOCIAL STRATEGIES

If someone is found to exhibit less and less of social competence as it is the case in many Nigerian public organizations including the police force, school institutions etc. Common sense supposedly believed that such origin was traceable to learning inadequacies. Places of learning form the capacity as a social strategic system for social competence. Through the school system, religious observance, culture and arts and sports the capacity of social strategy may be communicated.

The importance of social competence as a constituent of healthy social development cannot be over emphasized. If you want to measure Nigerian's mental health from the police force down to the elementary pupils study their social competence. Evidence on negative and positive social skill in people may emerge as follows:

- Maladaptive attitudinal outcomes (negative)
- Adaptive attitude (positive)
- Problem solving skills (positive)
- Fighting and hostile outcomes (negative)
- Interactional and collaboration outcomes (positive)
- Ineffective social functioning (negative)
- Effective social functioning (positive)
- Lack of self-control (negative)

- Self-control outcomes (positive)

- Inability to process information (negative)

- Ability to process information (positive)

How people choose their social goals will affect how they respond to a situation. A person of poor social interactions, who cannot exhibit positive social skill in some interactions, may need to see a counselor. Such people may be found to have excessive anxiety or impulsivity which is responsible for prohibiting them from responding with proper behavioral skills whether as a soldier, a police, a leader or a private person.

Now that it is clear that one of the biggest problems of Nigeria is how to manage their social and economic situations; what advice can be offered to help such situations?

Looking at such situation the multi-ethnic skills and talents in Nigeria becomes a very indispensable factor to measure how fast Nigeria would prosper if managed by wiser leadership. This includes broadening the scope of social and economic process in every state in Nigeria including the many languages.

The three main processes considered here are the social, cultural and economic. Imagine the Whiteman had good knowledge of how social life and culture of those living around the Niger area was organized during the pre-Nigerian colonial history. The Whiteman acknowledged that the people had their social life which is explained in their culture and religion. Their creative products enriched their environment and provided means of livelihood for them. These three processes importantly encouraged interactions among the people from the east, west, north and south of the territory. That may have given the Whiteman the spur to reason on the line of merging the regions under indirect rule system.

For the past fifty years Nigerians were bent on doing political stuff which either did not recognize the effort or were ignorant of the fact that the Whiteman did marvelous work in Nigeria. The slave trade happened on the pre-colonial Niger-area for about three hundred years. Could you imagine that even mosquito was the fiercest plague and factor fighting in behalf of the slave bearers against the White Slave Merchants? The mosquito bites quelled the insurgence of slave trade from the middle of the 17th century towards the moribund of the 18th century such that the inflow of the White Merchants was slowed down or stopped abruptly because of the great number who died as a result of mosquito bite.

The socializing process, the lifestyle and the cultural impact on the life of Nigerians cannot be fully discussed without looking at how the regions have served in the complementarities of one another. The slave trade was mainly concentrated on the eastern and western regions for whatever reasons that made it so. There are propositions that they were more industrious in the use of physical and mental labor.

- Consequently the eastern and western territories were more bearers of socialization because towards the beginning of the 19th century the people were already scattering off themselves across the north and beyond. They could equally learn new languages. The trait of learning new something and very smart is related to the quest to advent and invent. So in this situation the east and the west were supplementing (increase) for the north making it so that the north could not be separated from the wave of socialization and soon such trait became a measure of the economic process. Some fifty years before the Nigerian independence records had it that the east and the west were more reaching out for the "Western" elitist socializing culture. If that was the case; yet they did not leave the north behind. They wanted to make the north to compete equally and remain part of economic zone so that socialization, culture and economic may serve as complements to their humanly qualities.

Today people discuss Nigeria as a multi-ethnic and religious; rich and strong with variety; but not yet indivisible and one as in unity. This is why understanding the historical happenings and to situate them in their proper context is very important in order to make meaning of Nigerian social process, culture and economic activities and today's Nigerian lifestyle.

Dividing Nigeria may amount to sporadic war fare; social warfare, trade war, cultural warfare and confrontations. The best for Nigeria is to completely federalize; then her ethnic and cultural complementarities will emerge fully and the country would truly become the real giant of Africa.

CHAPTER 5

Proposed Leverage: Security-Socio-Political and Economic
FEDERALIZE AND MODERNIZE NIGERIA

Proposed leverage is a process of restoration. Give the regional states the full subsidiary power to develop themselves and they will contribute fully to the resources of the central government. May the president and the central government concentrate on issues of more central concern and take responsibility for those concerns so as to narrow the large and diverse jurisdiction of the federal concern in order for work to be easy. May the states concentrate on regional issues and take responsibility for that so that the culture of domino-effect on blames for irresponsibility and dereliction which has increasingly weakened the moral strength of the country would be avoided.

Modernize the Nigerian system of governance through adaptive federal model as it was the original design by the British considering the ethnic cleavage. This is a headline which intends to discuss the usefulness of Nigerianess in the type of federalism Nigeria needs. There is apparently no Nigerianess in the present federal republic which Nigeria is practicing. Nigeria may have to rethink, reappraise and adapt the full federalist model which is Nigerian in content in order to fast pedal her development and move as fast as other more developed countries. There are so many causes of lack and lagging behind in the current federal republic model:

- The Federal Center is the center of everything.
- Federal monopoly of opinion and decision making.
- The capitalist economic model is un-standardized and unstable because is regulated by the center.
- The socialist economic model is unpredictable because policies are not just central but lacks feasibility studies.
- The security systems local and federal are below conventional standard and they prevail with domino-effect on blames for irresponsibility and dereliction so that nobody is held responsible at the end of the day and no efficient command is followed; which is tantamount to systemic corruption.
- The will and yearning of the people is not met and there is massive lack of medium of feedback and communication and sense of belonging and responsibility.

The modern federalism is a system of government which was created as a reaction or was formed to make a difference from the type of system which the British established for themselves as the British Unitary System. The system is unique with Great Britain because of its advancement and its political organization.

The British Unitary System of government is the type in which power of governance is located on the central government in London.

The concept of a federal union of states was exemplified in the Constitution of the United States of the 1787. This was a milestone difference in the modern concept of system of governance.

THE CONSTITUTIONAL SYSTEM NATIONS

The essence of constitutionalism is the control of power and its distribution among several state organs or offices in such a way that they are each subjected to reciprocal controls and forced to cooperate in formulating the will of the state. The examples of countries running the modern federal system of government are: The United States and Canada, Germany and Russia, Argentina, Brazil and Mexico, Switzerland, Australia and India. Nigeria is supposedly one of these countries. By the time you finished reading this book you will discover why there is doubt concerning Nigerian constitutional system and why Nigeria is so backward and the suggestions that need to be delivered to move it forward; not just to move forward but to compete with the developed world. Is Nigeria running a federal system or a republic? Is there any correlation, strong, direct and pragmatic between the Nigerian political order and the Nigerian socio-cultural order? It is not difficult to interpret. It is very simple to explain. Federal republic is a mockery to Nigerian civilization. It is a show of ignorance towards restoring the dignity and prestige of the nation. It is a political system that is set on kleptocracy.

The European Union (EU) and the United States may be taken as the leading example in the practice of modern federalism with the presence of their multi-state situation. Such setting may be expressed in the terms "the federal union of states" or states united by the common bond of federation.

THE FEDERAL SYSTEM

The federal system of governance is a workable and plausible system in large nations with very diverse populations or even with multi-ethnic groups like Nigeria.

The national government is clearly more powerful than those of their subdivisions, even though the constitutions delegate many powers and responsibilities to the sub-national units. In certain prescribed policy areas a state government may have a high degree of autonomy.

Effective government in the modern times in any form requires a pragmatic and workable method for distributing authority within the country.

The larger and more diverse the jurisdiction of the government the stronger the tendency towards a federal system, in which authority is "layered" or distributed among different levels. That explains why Nigeria should be fully federalized.

In countries with a relatively homogeneous population and with a common tradition, language, and sense of national history, the central governments may not be federal but unitary or republic, that is, they may retain most of the administrative power at the center. You could see why the Great Britain is the way it is. The United Kingdom otherwise known as Great Britain is made up of four countries or regions: England, Scotland, Wales and Northern Ireland. They are not multi-ethnic regions like Nigeria. Loosely allied autonomous states sometimes join together to create a type of central government known as a confederation, in which the central government exists only at the pleasure of the sovereign members.

CHARACTERISTICS OF DEMOCRATIC MODEL

- There is free participation and shared ideological direction
- Citizens believe in the proactive principle whereby everyone is motivated to act in support or in disagreement without biases or being intimidated
- Every hand on deck so that everybody is inspired to contribute one's initiative, talents, ability and knowledge as a commitment and obligation.
- Sense of belonging – citizens who participate in the affairs of their common life freely with pride of sense of belonging build healthier environment, live happier life and live longer life. Sense of belonging defines a person's participation within the group or in a society. Sense of belonging is important in building a healthy nation and in making a healthy people and in human development or organization, and in combating behavior problems, depression and suicide

and overdose of drugs. It is very important and has equal importance in child development starting from early training. As a child needs sense of belonging to develop in a healthy life so a nation needs sense of belonging to develop in terms of living in a securer and healthier environment.

Sense of belonging is important for one to be able to effectively participate in the network of development and leadership. "Sense of belonging can improve physical and mental health" (Cf. Dpt. Of Human Resources and Skills Development Canada).

In a Theory of Human Motivation in 1943, Abraham Maslow tagged "Sense of belonging" in the hierarchy of human needs to be the third most important need of every human being. But in the hierarchy of socio-political need sense of belong to citizens comes first. If this is true, it is also true that sense of belonging is one of the greatest needs for a nation to improve its dignity and leadership dynamics; identity, participation, productivity, prestige and leaders' common skill.

COMMITMENT-PROCESS OF DEMOCRATIZATION AND MODERNIZATION

Participation Dynamics: Hands-on

"Democracy does not require uniformity... it requires a basic sense of solidarity". (Barack Obama).

The Democratic Leadership, also known as participative leadership or shared leadership is a leadership style in which members takes participative role in deciding what is best for their future. That is why democracy reemphasizes equality and remains one of the best leadership styles with the highest productive advantage in the developed cultures.

High Lines in the Ideology of Sense of Belonging:

- Feeling of being secure
- Feeling of being recognized and cared for

- Feeling of being suitable or able to participate or give an opportunity or right to live
- Feeling of being liked/ loved and respected and protected

"Nations and people with more social support and feel more of a sense of belonging report less suicide, mental and depressive symptoms" (Cf. University of Michigan study).

"Adolescents who find group membership important and have a positive sense of group belonging have significantly fewer behavior problems than those who see group membership as very important, but do not have a positive sense of group belonging" (Cf. University of Rhode Island study).

Nigerians find group membership very important but they have come from a distorted time that made them feel less positive of group belonging. That is the background of so many agitations happening on the country. Nigerians want to live together; the Hausas love the Ibo, the Yorubas love the Ibo, the

Ibo loves the Hausas and Yorubas as well as the other groups; someone has to initiate the sense of belonging culture.

Lack of fostering of sense of belonging in any society might bring about unwanted influences that deter the development of the society. It makes greater sense to argue for sense of belonging as a necessary mechanism, dynamism and influence to modify and build the Nigerian society. Lack of sense of belonging brings about in Nigerian society the attitude of:

- I don't care
- I don't know
- I don't like
- I don't participate
- I don't belong
- I can't help etc.

Where this attitude is the case; and has come to stay for too long, it becomes increasingly difficult to know who to blame when things go wrong. And this is the source of domino-effect in blame game in the Nigerian situation. It is the attitude of people who willingly and unwilling make great efforts but in the end have nothing to account for their efforts.

Sense of Belonging in the Nigerian Socio-political Situation

Who represents sense of belonging in the Nigerian situation? It implies a people with a real leader with perception and emphasis on:

- Sense of purpose and duty
- Sense of Commitment
- Sense of dedication and patience
- Sense of accountability and transparency
- Sense of feed-back and attentive listening
- Sense of respect and love

Sense of belonging may help re-purpose the goals of the government and the leadership goals whereby citizens get to understand their own part in the realization of the goals of the nation.

This can be recognized as one of the essential resources and capital necessary for working in collaboration with the government as obligation and as a need; the absence of sense of belonging may be equal to aimless goal pursuit in governance or no government at all.

In modern governance one of the best leadership resources is the sense of belonging in which every citizen feels involved. This works in reciprocity for a common purpose of service that is rooted in a belief in the common ability as a tradition that aims at producing honest diligent and hard-working spirit for the building of a prestigious nation.

This may help in no small measure to oppose and uproot a sense of rootlessness, carelessness, laziness and spurious ethnic competition, agitation and crime; which is the main cause of Nigeria vicious social fragmentation, hatred and hypocrisy.

Another means of ensuring that citizens get even with sense of common ability and cohesion in the country, the State must encourage and protect the multi religious adherence as a right; the ethnic and cultural sharing, diversity and creativity as medium of cohesion and interaction in which peoples' actions may be shadowed and social problems identified and clarified as quickly as possible so that nobody has no place to belong. One of the social problems in Nigeria is that there are many who have no where they belong and no one cares what they do or what they think; just because they don't belong to the main stream or to the popular class.

Sense of belonging is recognized in the essential needs and the provision of basic and social facilities like neatness of environment, hospitals, schools, recreation centers, water, electricity, and good road net-works and markets as necessary infrastructure and not a luxury etc.

It includes proper prodding of young peoples' talents to raise the identity, participation and prestige of the nation. State governments may foster sense of belonging projects through reconstructing and modification of state programs.

The concern of the families, their religious creeds and attachment as they connect the state government should be within close shadow of the state aim to transform the fallen moral state of the society.

Sense of belonging produces "team spirit". The project of developing a nation always comes with developing the mind of a people in line with clarified vision and common value of the nation. It must be recognized that team spirit is the most elaborate projects aimed at producing transformational leaders; from team spirit leaders who have the capacity to transform environments and people emerges.

Sense of belonging precedes attachment and identity of history; without which every memory of solidarity and identity is a shallow story of the past. If one does not have sense of belonging; history and the past would not mean any value or would not mean so much or there would be no positive reference to history when sense of belonging is lost. If sense of belonging is lost, history is as well lost.

Sense of belonging gives confidence this can be read from the French soccer world cup squad in 2018 in which African French citizens dominated the competition and finally brought the victory from the tournament to France; although their fellow African counterparts could not survive the early stage of the tournament.

Sense of belonging reinforces the solidarity that overcomes troubling times and the mutual enjoyment of prosperity. Sense of identity and solidarity is one great concern that brings additional value and makes effective economy. To grow a nation's economy a people must be able to grow in their sense of identity and solidarity and develop a focus resources project; with such transformational vision and spirit which reflect practically in work behavior; a new nation is born. The product of sense of identity, sacrifice and solidarity is that factor which leads people to do proudly in the name of their country.

Building optimism into people enhances identity and solidarity. The identity of a people defines how positive and optimistic they are toward their challenging future. That has to do also with a greater knowledge and sense of their history and sacrifice.

Sense of justice and fairness is very important in building history and also as part of belongingness, it comes with the knowledge and ability to do things for others – to remain poor while make others rich just like a good teacher, a good farmer, a good physician etc. A citizen with better sense of justice, sacrifice and fairness remains a model who leaves great impact on the fellow citizens. Such are models who encourage other citizens on how to surmount difficulties and challenges in building a historical nation and leave pace of success and transformational attitude as reference point for the future generation. The essence of sense of justice, sacrifice and fairness is to produce people with spirit and valor to stand up in the interest of others.

The Nigerian government should consider developing schemes that would promote sense of belonging as a good strategy beginning from rural communities; communicating and taking the task of re-teaching the spirit of sacrifice and knowledge and transformational attitude toward work to create an idea whereby people in the rural area can enjoy the same comfort as those in the city. By this the crises in the overcrowded cities would be mitigated.

Engaging people in the rural area on partnership engagement and encourage citizens to join partnership ventures where they share their benefit mutually is a great means of achieving difficult things and transforming the environment is a great idea and development.

Rural residents' awareness of their needs increases their transformational attitude. There is no better way of creating such awareness unless through effective communication and feedback. A continual teaching and re-teaching concerning what makes life livable and valuable and how to preserve the infrastructures of development is the communal mind of growing in knowledge of need.

Security and feedback is one great need among citizens. Their participation and feedback in their security project increases their transformational effort and communal mind.

Confidence towards the leadership mechanism helps to support communal health system and help to increase mutual effort. Confidence makes for optimal level of energy to operate but that has to be when there is familiarity. Confidence is built when people get familiar with the leadership system or leader personnel. Every leader-follower confidence is built on familiarity.

Sense of Belonging: Leaders' Social Competence

The present system of government in Nigeria and the present constitution have failed to give the people sense of belonging. In the hierarchy of human and political needs sense of belonging comes not as private pursuit alone but as communal prioritized value in the items to be pursued by a real leader as a social competence. A real leader spreads the uniting dynamics of belongingness. Nigeria is looking forward among other things for a real leader who will prioritize sense of belonging with citizens.

A sense of belonging is in relation with common body or in acceptance with a belonged group or in connection with some other participants where someone belongs or operates. It means the sentiment or feeling that a person is connected and accepted or is meaningfully represented within one's group, for instance one's family or one's country; everybody's presence and person makes real meaning in such unifying dynamic leadership. Nigeria must have to reform its constitution in order to get to value belongingness among citizens and as its social-communal competence. This may bring about the identity of every person and add value to the identity of every citizen. Sense of belonging would redeem the common value and identity of the country in general and the citizen if properly understood.

Identity Diversity Dynamics

Every citizen by common right has a stake in the dynamic purposefulness or sense of purpose as a stake. Sense of belonging is connected with who a person is and how a person identifies with either a smaller group or a larger group in which one operates. Such sensitivity influences the person's ability to act in more positive and beneficial ways.

DECENTRALIZE THE COMMAND SOURCE OF THE NIGERIAN POLICE FORCE

The Nigerian centralized leadership culture drains human resources and siphon assets to the advantage of the center while the state units and the community units are left under-resourced and undeveloped.

The Nigerian Security System

The Nigerian security system, precisely the policing is weak to the miasma of insurgence, home terrorism, abduction, kidnapping, theft, and armed robbery etc. Huge amount of money is being wasted by the Federal Government on crime control projects, sophisticated weapons, strategic instructions, training and all the rest of it. What is the impact of psychological training and the psychology behind the image crisis of policing? There appears to be high level of insecurity in Nigeria both in the city and in the rural areas? There are measures individuals have taken to reduce at least the frequency of falling prey to the criminals or letting one's belongings lose to the lifters or pickpockets. The same amount of sense of security is required by the policing organization to keep the environment rid of criminals; but one little thing more is required. Everybody has to be involved in the sensitization in order to make sense of security a culture and to sustain a steady mode of trust, reliance, confidence and safety in the environment especially in the fast developing environment like Nigeria. The rural areas and communities do not need high level of professional police presence to describe how crimes happen and who were behind them. If the governing body can look into these honestly one would know that money is being wasted in doing big security projects while some less expensive and very necessary things are left undone.

What is the Problem of the Nigerian Police Force?

What is the problem of the Nigerian Police? Is it lack of education, poor training scheme, lack of discretion, poor intelligence competence, poor supervision or all of the above?

The problem of insecurity and policing in Nigeria in the city and in the rural areas is on exponential increase. Among the institutional setbacks of the Nigerian Police force is:

- Lose of public trust on police force
- Bribery and corruption
- Politicization
- Lack of administrative will
- Weak supervision
- Unreasonable compromise
- The culture of impunity
- Lack of professional will
- Arbitrary arrests
- Lack of due process
- Lack of understanding and commitment
- Lack of sufficient training
- Dereliction and negligence

- Unreasonable professional compromise and the culture of domino-effect as blame game

The Historic Footprints in Police Miscreant

The Nigerian Police Force can still do better in spite of its past history with the presence of the White Imperial influence which made stooge and distrust of the indigene police constables and subject them to series of embarrassment; and such was the origin of condition of distrust to the security agents. But such situation can still be overcome through the strong professional will and adaptation and integral training.

The Nigerian – Biafran war ended, throwing in the wind of disarray; even the accountability value of security organizations, army, police etc was jettisoned; worse in the centralizing of the Nigerian governance. The next was the military leadership malpractices in Nigeria which smeared the Nigerian Police Force with bad influence; the continuation of which still felt under the democratic rule up to now. The sad history of law enforcement organizations in Nigeria is a blistering history with relative absence of professional and functional accountability.

There is so much politicization going on directed to the central leadership of the Nigerian Police Force and one of the epic centers of the Nigerian corrupt political practices. This happens to the advantage of the policing miscreant. This is the policing blame game; the domino-effect culture which gave rise to corruption, compromise, dereliction and impunity,

There is Need for Milestone Police Reform

There is need for governance reforms from the center to the states level. There is need for police reforms. How may the Nigerian Police force be reformed to gain the public trust, depoliticized and be rid of corruption?

The success of every civil society or every institution is built on how such institution is able to appreciate its challenges, understand them and applied the experience towards effective commitment for the future success.

The Police Force can still reform and build community trust and restore confidence.

Completely federalizing Nigeria is the best option to correct the overly mistakes and injury done to the Nigerian sociopolitical reality. This in practical terms means decentralizing the leadership of the law enforcement systems to the power of the States.

The States Sector

By empowering the States level commands there would be greater familiarity and greater sense of security between the citizens and the law enforcement agents. This would checkmate excessive politicization and professional compromise.

By decentralizing the Nigerian Police Force to the States the whole blistering political effort that has ruined the country's custodian agents of security and law enforcement will come to an end because it would be easier to identify the roots of the policing miscreants and that would end the domino-effect of blame game.

In order to improve security effectiveness through Nigerian Police Force the States should have the command source, supervision source, accountability and responsibility to meet the security needs of the citizens; this requires some restructuring of the system of governance of the Nigerian Police Force from the center to the States.

The Community Sector

To encourage community based interactive awareness between the police and the community on greater sense of security the community would have to be fully involved in order to enforce proper community based accountability and responsibility which is necessary to ease problem solving in the community level. This is also because a lot of corrupt practices are hidden under the bureaucratic bottlenecks which delays important priority decisions from federal center to the states.

DECONGEST THE CENTER

The system of government of Nigeria – the mixture of unitary and federal did influence its economic structure that the center of government was the center of everything; and such was the reason of the congestion of the center. And for over five decades of the independence the center has suffered the congestion of economy, politics, education, manpower, investment, industries, employment, international negotiation and population figure doctoring etc.

One of the reasons for transferring the capital territory from Lagos to Abuja was to decongest Lagos as the center of commerce which was also the center of industries and the center for international engagements and of course the center of everything.

The country inherited Lagos as the birth place of the unitary system of government from Great Britain and made a slight reform into a Federal Republic in which the tenets of unitary system was still in dictation of the principles where the country's developmental landscapes were centrally determined and contrary to the ideal and modern developmental structure.

The central government decides the plan, draw the plans, fund the plans and implement the programs. The system absolutized the essence and value of development such that the developmental programs of the entire country were centrally fixed. The easily inferred insinuations were that:

- Development was fixed

- Market was fixed

- Money was fixed

- Commerce both local and foreign was fixed

- Competition both local and foreign was fixed
- Principle of subsidiarity for the states was fixed
- Everything could be stage managed including election results.

That can be seen in the state governors' scramble to shuttle to and from Abuja the capital territory for collection of allocation and quota. The system leaves survival on the hands of the few who were opportune to wangle their way up to the center and the palace of power.

DYNAMICS OF THE PRINCIPLE OF SUBSIDIARY GOVERNANCE

The creation of federal states would automatically create 36 central development units in centers of finance, development, commerce and competition. If states were given the opportunity to manage what they have been given as natural resources. The opportunity cost of what they do not have could lead them to learn how to lean on those states that have what others do not have. This is itself an economic solidarity spot by global diversity. This may control extravagant spending on unimportant programs. The subsidiarity principle has increasing advantage in the program of federalizing the Nigerian system of governance through economic solidarity and dependence between one state and another which spot the indispensability of unity in diversity among states.

APPENDIX

In 1946, the British divided the Southern Region into the Western Region and the Eastern Region. Each government was entitled to collect royalties from resources extracted within its area.

This changed in 1956 when Shell-BP found large petroleum deposits in the Eastern region. A Commission led by Jeremy Raisman and Ronald Tress determined that resource royalties would now enter a "Distributable Pools Account" with the money split between different parts of government (50% to region of origin, 20% to federal government, 30% to other regions). This method can still be considered in the win-win conflict resolution conference in order to quell agitation concerning resources in Nigeria.

The GDP of Nigerian grew 1.9% in 2018 compared to 2017. The GDP per capita of Nigerian in 2018 was $2,028. It was $1,972 in 2017. In 2008 the GDP per capita was $2,234. Nigerian GDP per capita has shown that Nigerian population belongs to the low level of affluence compared to the about 196 countries. https://countryeconomy.com/gdp/nigeria

Below are the 36 States in Nigeria and their GDP for the year 2015 compliment, and courtesy of the National Bureau of Statistics and Kingmakers.

Per Capita: Using the word per capita in analyzing the GDP explains the highest income for each person in the population of a state whose GDP is shown.

Rank	State	GDP (US$)	GDP Per Capita (US$)	Annual GDP Growth Rate
1	Lagos	50,8346,417,32	4182	9.70%
2	River	33,697,048,223	4773	11%
3	Oyo	27,251,181,227	3596	12.60%
4	Delta	20,795,033,384	3791	4.60%
5	Ogun	18,478,286,455	3660	13.80%
6	Imo	18,316,956,593	3497	5.40%
7	Kano	16,060,452,398	1269	5.50%
8	Edo	14690747744	3563	4.60%
9	Akwa Ibom	14,394,934,514	2717	5.50%
10	Kaduna	14,383,292,476	1796	7.10%
11	Cross River	12,260,535,098	3264	6.20%
12	Abia	11,954,295,628	3295	7%
13	Benue	11,463,880,127	2057	12.10%
14	Ondo	10,986,434,580	2423	6%
15	OSun	10,02,328,8394	2,199	7.30%
16	Katsina	8,715,622,952	1,147	7.90%
17	FCT Abuja	8,709,940,093	2,682	12.10%
18	Anambra	8,551,191,419	1,591	5%
19	Zamfara	7,758,988,606	1,774	14%
20	Niger	7,315,871,445	1,362	4.10%
21	Plateau	6,696,670,490	1,638	5.90%
22	Kogi	6,423,622,338	1,480	7.40%
23	Ebonyi	6,084,268,690	2,172	18.80%
24	Sokoto	5,957,303,706	1,228	4.40%
25	Enugu	5,860,198,009	1,369	6.30%
26	Borno	5,770,088,940	1,019	2.90%
27	Bayelsa	5,517,415,395	2,493	5.30%
28	Kwara	5,028,001,438	1,623	6%
29	Bauchi	4,351,446,293	686	-0.70%
30	Kebbi	4,265,932,882	991	5.50%
31	Jigawa	4,200,635,064	742	7.30%

32	Nasarawa	4,060,789,133	1,658	6.60%
33	Adamawa	3,995,509,662	968	-1.70%
34	Ekiti	3,592,364,990	1,133	5.10%
35	Yobe	2,261,353,875	711	2.70%
36	Gombe	2,162,199,971	685	-1.80%
37	Taraba	1,908,888,779	641	-8.80%

A commonsense observation of the Gross Domestic Products below explains the fact that the workforce of the nation is cloistered within a certain territory while other territories were disadvantaged. On the same fact; per capita as reflects on the distribution of monthly salary shows that Nigerian employees live from the tooth of their skin to make ends meet in relation with the revealed data on cost of living. From the GDP table it is easy to read why some states are poor while some are rich. It is also easy to read the increasing disproportion of the rich and poor which is the reason of the decline of the aggregation of wealth. The paradigm is that the widening of the gap between the rich and the poor depletes the total wealth of any country.

(Cf. the Swiss Bank's annual global wealth report – Philippines 2017).

The World Bank made a classification of the world's economies in four income categories:

- High
- Upper-middle
- Lower-middle and
- Low

The World Bank defines middle-income countries from their economies as those countries with a Gross National Income (GNI) per capita between $1,026 and $12,475. This classification or categorization would help the World Bank on the kind of financial and economic development services to be provided for countries. Middle-income countries comprise of a large portion of the world's population and economic activities. These countries are necessary for global economic growth. This is the category Nigeria belongs. The category distinguished

Nigeria as one of the countries considered as key to global development. The characteristics speak as such that Nigeria is not considered as a poor country. Nigeria is only poor when it comes to the inability of their leaders to put into full activity their resources. So this book repeats the statement with the (MIC); Nigeria is not a poor country. Lower-middle-income economies have per capita GNIs between $1,026 and $3,955, while upper-middle economies have per capita GNIs between $3,956 and $12,475. (https://www.macrotrends.net/countries/NGA/nigeria/gni-per-capita).

The feature of poverty in Nigeria can be seen in the inability to provide citizens with the essential services like, water, electricity, roads, healthcare and schools.

> "Sustainable growth and development in MICs have positive spillovers to the rest of the world. Examples are poverty reduction, international financial stability, and global cross-border issues, including climate change, sustainable energy development, food and water security, and international trade". (Cf. World Bank on middle-income economies).

Essentially the following factors can influence a country's (GNI) growth:

- Inflation
- Exchange rates and
- Population

Salary Earning in Nigeria

From the table of salary distribution in Nigeria it can be viewed that the average earner in Nigeria gets a salary of more or less three hundred and thirty nine thousand naira per month.

https://medium.com/kingmakers/how-we-projected-the-gdp-for-states-in-nigeria-5ccc5e2c85f7

Average Monthly & Average Yearly Salary in Nigeria 2020

Low	Average	High
Monthly N85,700	Monthly N339,000	Monthly N1,510,000
Yearly 1,030,000	Yearly 4,060,000	Yearly 18,100,000

How much is the take home of an average worker in Nigeria per month or what is the monthly salary of an average worker in Nigeria? Approximately N339, 000 is the salary of an average person working in Nigeria. There is salary difference in different jobs and in different places.

The Standard of Living in Nigeria

Considering from the data on the three categorical groups of salary: the low, average and high; it is not so easy to come up with a yardstick to measure standard of living in relation with one's income or salary. It appears there is no common parameter to measure standard of living in Nigeria because standard of living in Nigeria is influenced by factors like, place of work, lifestyle, location, income/salary, dependency ratio and of course accurate gouge of population. So apparently what exists is individual standard of living which is known to be generally low and below average with reference to the volume of people within the low and average income category. The standard of life which an average Nigerian with the minimum wage may be able to access may be very low considering the basic life needs. It is the fact that the average cost of living is relatively higher than the average income of Nigerians.

A minimum wage earner and an average Nigerian should be able to access such life basic needs like:

- Fairly comfortable shelter
- Good food
- Healthcare
- Clean water
- Electricity

A cost of living survey made in 2014 captured that Abuja and Lagos rank 25th and 36th respectively as most expensive cities in the world.

The followings are the major sources of the Federal Government of Nigeria revenue:

- Crude oil sales; NNPC petroleum sales, gas, proceeds from national and international oil companies.

- Revenues from federal taxes, levies, agricultural sector, aviation, federal examination fees, other forms of license fees, import duties and tariffs etc.

- External borrowing and foreign aids etc.

REFERENCES

https://www.pulse.ng/lifestyle/food-travel/why-we-struck-reviewing-the-book-that-tells-us-about-nigerias-first-coup-detat/9rrfwhq

https://www.stearsng.com/article/is-the-nigerian-economy-capitalist-socialist-or-mixed

https://en.wikipedia.org/wiki/1959_Nigerian_general_election

https://api.parliament.uk/historic-hansard/commons/1960/jul/15/nigeria-independence-bill

https://en.wikipedia.org/wiki/Murtala_Mohammed

https://www.facebook.com/notes/asiwaju-bola-ahmed-tinubu/exclusive-interview-with-gmb-buhari-speaks-to-the-sun-newspaper/409638299105506/

https://www.vanguardngr.com/2018/08/why-zik-escaped-death-in-1966/

http://www.gamji.com/nowa/news103.htp

https://web.archive.org/web/20070629231635/htp:/kwenu.com/publications/siollun/1966_coup1.htm

http://www.photius.com/countries/nigeria/government/nigeria_government_the_1966_coups_civi-10021.html

http://allafrica.com/stories/201007200259.html

http://info-naija-blogspat.com/2009/03/history-of-coup-detat-in-nigeria.html

http://www.dawodu.com/buhari.htm

http://www.dawodu.com/siollun30htm

http://www.gamji.com/sanusi/sanusi26.htm

http://allafrica.com/stories/201009140173.html

https://punchng.com/breaking-inec-declares-buhari-winner-of-2019-presidential-election/

https://www.theguardian.com/world2015/mar/31/muhammadu-buhari-military-dictator-nigeria-new-democratic-president

https://web.archive.org/web/20190218031931/https:/www.britannica.com/biography/muhammadu-buhari

Obotetukudo, Solomon (2011). The Inaugural Addresses and Ascension Speeches of Nigerian Elected and Non elected presidents and prime minister from 1960 -2010. University Press of America. p. 90.

http://www.vanguardngr.com/2012/11/the-nigerian-defence-academy-a-pioneer-cadets-memoir/#sthash0o9A0qM0

Agbese, Dan (2012). Ibrahim Babangida: The Military, Power and Politics. Adonis & Abbey Publishers, 2012. pp. 48–49. ISBN 978-1-906704-96-4.

https://books.google.com/?id=q/A44AAAAj&pg=PA235&jpg=PA235&dq=teshie%20military%20nmtc%20lucham&f=false

Solomon Williams Obotetukudo (2010). The Inaugural Addresses and Ascension Speeches of Nigerian Elected and Non-Elected Presidents and Prime Minister, 1960–2010. University Press of America. pp. 91–92.

http://allafrica.com/stories/201501020034html

(https://en.wikipedia.org/wiki/Flora_Shaw,_Lady_Lugard)

https://thecommonwealth.org/our-member-countries/nigeria/constitution-politics

https://www.mouau.edu.ng//index.php/node/134

http://www.nigeriaroute.com/state-structure.php

https://www.pulse.nig/news/local/nigerian-states-this-is-how-the-36-states-were-created/mdtnq3e

Alapiki, Henry; E (2005). "State Creation in Nigeria: Failed Approaches to National Integration and Local Autonomy".

https://doi.org/10.1353/arw.2006.0003

https://www.jstor.org/stable/20065139

https://www.nnpcgroup.com/NNPCBusiness/Businessinformation/OilGasinNigeria/IndustryHistory.aspx

"Nigeria's Oil Production on Increase." *Afro-American* (1893–1988): 16. 16 December 1978.

Matthews, Martin P. *Nigeria: current issues and historical background.* p. 121.

http://www.refworld.org/docid3ae6ab5d3c.html

https://web.archive.org/web/20150120004503/http:naijapolitica.com/2014/12/04/the-untold-tales-of-gen-buhari-a-must-read/

https://www.bbc.co.uk//news/world-africa-12890807

http://www.africa.upenn.edu/Urgent_Action/apic_52396html

Nwachuku, Levi Akalazu; G. N. Uzoigwe (2004). *Troubled Journey: Nigeria Since the Civil War. University Press of America.* p. 192.

https://books.google.com/?id=hts6GpM4zDMC&pg=PA122&lpg=PA122&dp=buhari+imf#v=onepage&q=buhari%20imf&f=false

https://www.nytimes.com/1984/08/10/world/nigeria-s-discipline-campaign-nt-sparing-the-rod-html

https://web.archive.org/web/20150120113947/http://www.abiyamo.com/muhammadu-buhari-nigerias-strictest-leader/7/

http://saharareporters.com/2007/01/14/crimes-buhari-wole-soyinka

Toyin Falola; Matthew M. Heaton (2008). A History of Nigeria. Cambridge University Press. p. 271.

http://www.jstor.org/stable/20042576

http://www.dawodu.com/siollun3htm

http://news.bbc.co.uk//1/hi/world/Africa/6508055.stm

http://news.bbc.co.uk/2/hi/africa/6584393.stm

http://allafrica.com/stories/201003180375.htm

http://www.aljazeera.com/indepth/opinion/2914/12/will-muhammadu-buhari-be-niger-2014123191647111939.html

http://www.vanguardngr.com/2011/10/post-election-violence-fg-panel-report-indict-buhari/

http://www.voanews.com/content/nigeria-opposition-leader-vows-to-improve-security/2557090.html

http://freebeacon.com/issues/david-axelrods-political-consulting-firm-far-more-involved-in-nigeria-election-than-previously-disclosed/

http://www.afria-confidential.com/article/id/11829/political_schism_hit_recovery_and_reform

https://www.ft.com/content/2f7d3a24-66eb-11e7-8526-7b38dcaef614

https://web.archive.org/web/20170206165902/http:/www.internationallawoffice.com/com/Newsletters/White-Collar-Crime/Nigeria/sofunde-Osakwe-Ogundipe-Belgore/Federal-Ministery-of-finance-introduces-new-whistleblowing-initiative

https://allafrica.com/stories/201805290530.html

http://www.xinhuanet.com/english/2019-12/20/c_138646834.htm

https://www.channelstv.com/2020/01/23/transparency-international-scores-nigeria-low-on-corruption-perception-index/

https://www.thecable.ng/breaking-nigeria-ranks-lower-on-transparency-internationals-corruption-index

Department of Education, Science and Training 2005, *National Framework for values education in Australian schools*, Commonwealth of Australia, Canberra

Dovre, PJ 2007, 'From Aristotle to Angelou: best practices in character education', *Education Next*, Spring 2007, 38–45

Hamston, J et al. 2010, *Giving voice to the impacts of values education: The final report of the Values in action schools project*, Education Services Australia, Carlton South

Knight, GR 1998, *Philosophy & Education: An introduction in Christian perspective*, Andrews University Press, Berrien Springs, Michigan

. https://www.legit.ng/1138446-jonathan-lists-10-achievements-president-dares-critics-show-records-achievem.html

https://www.legit.ng/291232-goodluck-jonathan-administration.html: https://www.legit.ng/291232-goodluck-jonathan-administration.html

https://www.investopedia.com/terms/h/humancapital.asp

https://en.wikipedia.org/wiki/Socioeconomics

https://en.wikipedia.org/wiki/Social_Thinking

https://en.wikipedia.org/wiki/Social_competence

Gray Carol (2010) The New Social Stories Book. Smith – Myles, Trautman & Schelven, Brenda (2004) The Hidden Curriculum. Autism Asperger. Dunn – Buron & Curtis, Kari (2003) The Incredible 5 – Point Scale – Autism Asperger Publishing. Attwood, Tony. "Tony Attwood" The Complete Guide to Aspergers. Semrud- Clikeman, M. (2007) Social Competence in Children. New York, NY: Spinger Science+Business Media.

Made in the USA
Columbia, SC
09 October 2020